Tales From the Hills

SECRETS OF THE STAFFORDSHIRE MOORLANDS

Bill Cawley

LEB
Books

First published in Great Britain in 2015 by LEB Books, a division of
LEB Ltd, 57 Orrell Lane, Liverpool L9 8BX

ISBN 978-0-9573141-9-1

British Library Cataloguing in Publication Data.
A catalogue record for this book is available from the British
Library.

Designed by Paul Etherington.

Dedicated to
Mavis, Cathy and Phoebe

ACKNOWLEDGEMENTS

The Leek Post and Times, Doug Pickford,
Ann Charlesworth, Gus Brain, Rose Baxter,
Simon Daniels, Paul Etherington and Nick Broadhead.

PHOTOGRAPHIC CREDITS

Front cover: Brett Trafford
Leek Market Place and Nicholson Institute: Leek Library
Mark Twain, The Green Knight, The Great Comet of 1680,
early aeronauts and the Battle of Waterloo: via
WikiCommons.

Tales From the Hills

SECRETS
OF THE
STAFFORDSHIRE
MOORLANDS

FOREWORD

Leek and the surrounding moorlands never fail to surprise and to delight. The awe-inspiring landscape of North Staffordshire enshrines the historic treasures of its past and acts as a magnet for thinkers, movers and shakers ... not to mention romantics both old and new and those who are not afraid to be themselves.

This has been the land of men and women who have helped shape the destiny of us all and who have left their legacies in the arts, politics, literature and the odd and unusual. Just why it should be thus may have something to do with the hidden beauty of the now and then of the place as well as the here and now. It could be put down to the rugged rural grandeur and ragged urban straggle or maybe that it has always been an oasis of sanity in an insane world.

Perhaps I am biased, but it does not alter the way it is. Leek and the Moorlands is a special place and has drawn special people for many a year. So thank goodness William (Bill) Cawley has lassoed many of these folk together and, as a consequence, is able to present them in an entertaining and commendable fashion within these pages.

He is an entertaining and worthy fellow himself – a *Mastermind* mastermind and a *University Challenge* challenger, a newspaper columnist and a regular leader of ghostly walks around the Queen of the Moorlands – and a continual seeker of facts and realities. A perfect person for the task in hand.

I first came across Bill when, as editor of the *Leek Post and Times*, I spoke to him about his political interests and happenings. Later, he came to my office armed with research he had carried out on literary connections of the Moorlands. Our acquaintance grew from there and once he was given access to the files of the local paper dating back more than 140 years he was in his element. He practically lived in that part of the office building, scouring the archives for this and for that. He was, and still is, in his element, and his regular articles for the newspaper testify to his popularity.

I can vouch for the vast amount of work he has put into compiling the stories that follow. Enjoy.

Doug Pickford

CONTENTS

AUTHOR'S
INTRODUCTION

It is a few years now since I began to write regularly for local newspapers. When I started my weekly column I had a number of intentions in mind. Firstly, the articles I wrote would try to link events in the past with contemporary issues. The shadows of the past all too frequently have an impact on present issues.

It is illuminating to see accounts in the past that have a modern day resonance, whether it be how to tackle poverty, the role of women or the lot of the common soldier in war. Over time I have found instances from the distant past which could be taken from newspapers today.

A second hope was to try to include many of the communities of the Staffordshire Moorlands. There are many villages and towns that make up the Staffordshire Moorlands and, in the course of the three years I was writing *Ghostwriter,* I included many of them in my articles. I have responded to requests from members of the public to include a story about a subject that interests them.

This can sometimes be challenging as often there is little in the archives, especially concerning the smaller settlements. In the case of the canal side hamlet Denford, this proved particularly taxing, although an opportunity arose following a conversation I had with a resident about the destruction of water vole in the area. This was caused by American mink, which had been released into the area with disastrous results for local wild life.

During this period I have relished discovering some of the 'lost' stories of the area. Finding the account of the 19th century hoarder, Bowcock, from Leek was a particularly enjoyable discovery. It was also a pleasure to come across the account of a young WH Auden discovering the industrial heritage of the Churnet Valley. I have been helped in my searches by use of the archive at the William Salt Library in Stafford and also more recently the on-line British Newspaper Archive which has proved an invaluable resource.

I also feel that, given the isolation and the poor transport of the area, the Staffordshire Moorlands has a rich and varied font of stories, many of them unknown to the modern reader. This is especially true of the period in Leek's history just before the First World war when many renowned writers and speakers passed through the town. The account of Oscar Wilde visiting the area to give a public lecture is quite well known, but the long association that John Betjeman had with Leek is perhaps less so. My researches also uncovered the connection that Leek had with Toussaint L'Overture, the leader of the Haitian Revolution. They also bought to the public attention a man who witnessed the execution of John Brown, who is considered an early leader in the independence movement in Sri Lanka. It was quite a pleasure to discover a local link to wider political and cultural development in different parts of the world

What makes the area attractive is the splendid landscape of the Staffordshire Moorlands which has played a part in some of the stories I have uncovered. Some years ago, I came across a book by WP Wincutt, a former priest in Leek who, writing in the 1950s, wrote of the special atmosphere of the area:

'Leek is not the kind of industrial town one finds in the south, whose industries have been transported from elsewhere, where factories have arisen in the fields as if by the waving of a magic wand. Its industrialism is the logical culmination of its history, and has not disturbed in the least the spirit of the place. The machines used by its people are merely the equivalent of their forefathers' 'bees'. The Leek demons look down from the moors upon the smoking mill-chimneys of the little town in the valley with perfect equanimity. They know well that the substitution of the power looms for hand looms has not altered the attitude of the Leek people towards them one whit. The Horseman, the Mermaid and the various Black Dogs still thrive in the imagination of the people of the town. And the fairies have not departed, but simply changed their names. No doubt they have grown tired of the nonsense talked of them by poets, and have reappeared in their original crudity as poltergeists. And the witches of Leek have changed their methods. They now deal in crystal globes instead of incantations'.

The legends of the Moorlands say something about the way the scenery has an impact upon the imagination, which can become, on occasion, a little too intoxicating. I recall a Leek librarian recounting to me a story her grandfather, a local farmer, told her. As they stood round a bonfire one autumn evening, years ago, he told her of a headless horseman rode the moors around Onecote. Suddenly they heard what sounded like a horse trotting down a nearby lane. The sound got closer and closer and the young girl shivered in fear and, at that very moment, a van with a flat tyre came into view.

Bill Cawley

July 2015

BOWCOCK:
A 'VISIONARY' OF
KILN LANE

Anyone who thinks that compulsive hoarding is a new phenomenon as revealed in television programmes, might like to hear of the case of George Bowcock of Kiln Lane.

I would go as far as to say that Bowcock might be one of the earliest accounts of the compulsive disorder, predating the case of the New York Collyer brothers by nearly 60 years.

The curious affair of Bowcock came to public notice in the 1870s when his activities were first investigated by the authorities. Leek's sanitary commission asked him to clear up his 'treasure house,' as he styled it, in 1873. George had 'by many years patient toil succeeded in amassing a heterogeneous collection of curiosities the like of which a man would never expect to see in the course of a lifetimes travel'.

The old man had assembled the collection in caves and passages around Kiln Lane, but he was ordered to clean it up and the material was carted away. Nothing daunted, he started again at 125 Mill Street, long since demolished, as he reported to a journalist that he intended to gather another collection "of such gigantic proportions to cast all other collections in the shade".

In a visionary statement, George "dreamed of a future world in which old pots grew on apple trees and there were mines of old cans, wheels, bottles, and crockery and where the whole world was engaged in an occupation collecting as much rubbish they could find room and a man's blissful or wretched state depended on what he collected".

George seems to have had the obsessive desire of people in the 21st century to acquire an assortment of stuff. Perhaps a large statue of him could be erected naturally from re-cycled materials in Brough Park? However, it proved too much for townspeople then and he was taken to court by Inspector Farrow for collecting rubbish 'injurious to health' in 1876.

Shortly before the rubbish was removed, a reporter called on George. He climbed into the house making his way through 'an assortment of broken and cracked gallipots which encumbered the stairway'. Clothes were everywhere and in the bedroom George sat on a bench encircled by pots in which he was brewing herbs. His bed was surrounded by detritus, but that did not concern him. "I only sleep here, I eat at Selina Tatton's," he cheerfully remarked.

LAUGHING AT STEAM ENGINES — RUSHTON SPENCER, 1870

In May 1913, the area saw a visit from the Anglo-Argentinian writer, WH Hudson. He was at the peak of his powers, having produced a great many books on bird watching and nature either in Britain or on Latin America.

His most well known book *Green Mansions* was published in 1904 and often cited as the first ecological novel. Subtitled *A Romance of the Tropical Forest*, it is a mystical novel on the life of a forest child in the Amazonian jungle who is at one with the animals of the jungle. Hudson was collecting material on Axe Edge for a book *Adventures Among Birds*. He was not impressed by the locals, comparing them unfavourably with the more fiery Lancastrians. He blamed their lack of spirit and energy on Methodism.

'Moorlanders are not a happy looking or a lively people. They have colourless faces and for good looks compare badly with inhabitants of the adjoining districts,' he wrote. The farming methods were backward. 'The farmers depend mainly on their lean ill-fed cows for a livelihood: they make butter and feed a pig or two with the skim milk. They live on bacon and buttermilk themselves and bread which they make or buy, but vegetables and fruit are luxuries'.

'I asked several farmers why they did not cut bracken which was plentiful enough, to serve as bedding for cows, since they could not get straw. They answered that occasionally a farmer did so, but it was not a custom and they thought the cows did just as well without bedding at all!'

Hudson encountered the innate deep-rooted conservatism of the area. This entirely coincides with an account from a farmer, Tom Mullins, born in 1863 whose autobiography is included in a collection of writings of working people called *Useful Toil* published by Penguin in the 70s. Mullins, whose book was written when he was an old man, recounts walking to Leek market as a ten year old from his parents' farm at Rushton Spencer with a basket containing 200 eggs on one arm and another basket with 12 lbs of butter on the other.

In the 1870s Mullins records that the reaction of the locals when the first steam-powered farm machines arrived in the area was one of laughter! The farming methods described are not far removed from the medieval, with Mullins quoting a farmer who was so far opposed to anything modern that he even refused to use horses.

A CANNIBAL
ON THE LOOSE!

The saying 'Coming to Leek out of the noise' was still popular in the early 20th century. I wonder if anyone still uses it? It is a saying which has a history - a history that could not be more gruesome.

Most people in the early 21st century will have heard of the fictional exploits of Hannibal Lecter - the creation of the writer Thomas Harris - whose terrifying desire to eat human flesh has gripped modern audiences. Well, Leek played its part in a real case of cannibalism which dates from the end of the 18th century and it's from this case that the saying sprang. The basic details are outlined in the diary of the Rev Jonathan Wilson, Master of Congleton Grammar School and Vicar of Biddulph, which was published in 1876 in the *Leek Times* to mark the 100th anniversary of this most shocking murder.

'Saturday 23rd November 1776
While at dinner heard of a most abominable murder a woman cut into a score of pieces in Prester Fields Brook.

Sunday 24th November 1776
The murderer detected and lodged in the town hall.

Monday 25th November 1776
Sam Thorley the murderer sent to Chester.

Thursday 11th April 1777
At school, after dinner, the boys are given leave to go and see Sam Thorley drawn on the gibbet.'

Gibbeting a body after a hanging was a punishment reserved for the most heinous of crimes. The body would hang in a metal cage for a long time, the idea being that the horror of the image would act as a deterrent, warning people that they would suffer the same end if they acted criminally. At that time, pitch was used very successfully to preserve the body and there was a case in Warwickshire where the body of a man hanged in 1766 was still on display 60 years later.

How Sam Thorley came to deserve this fate, I will now tell. Samuel Thorley was not an intelligent man, being described by his contemporaries as "half thick". He was born in Astbury in the 1720s and up to the events of late 1776 led an unremarkable life. He worked as a labourer on local farms and carried on his life honestly. He jobbed about in the slaughter houses of Congleton carrying out the butchering of livestock, a skill that was to have terrible consequences. He was also employed to dig graves at Astbury.

On Wednesday 20th November 1776, Thorley came across Ann Smith, a well known tramping ballad singer, who had come to sing at the Lammas Fair in Congleton the following Friday.

Three days later her body was found dismembered in a ravine where the footpath crosses a brook called the Howty. The sight was made more terrible as early snow had fallen and the whiteness contrasted with the bloody remains of the woman.

Later on that Wednesday, Thorley was seen with a blood-stained apron which seemed to be full of pork. A witness, named Hannah Oakes, was approached by Thorley and was asked to boil up the 'pork' for his supper. He ate some and fell sick and she was told to feed the rest of the meat to the dogs. She acted otherwise and kept it back when she heard of the disappearance and murder of Ann Smith. She gave the meat to a constable who gave it to a local doctor named Reade who, on examining the meat, pronounced it to be human flesh.

Thorley's blood-stained appearance at first excited no suspicion on account of his employment as a butcher. He became excited when he heard people talk about the discovery of the body and made the statement to Hannah that will live on many years after his death: "Folks will be laying this job on to him and he would go to Leek out of the noise".

He went to Leek on the Sunday and was quickly caught by the constable and brought back to Congleton to be imprisoned prior to the trial at Chester.

It has been said the saying owes its rise and popularity to the self-incriminating remark of Thorley. What led to the horrible fate of Ann Smith?

Thorley admitted all at the trial and gave an account of the fateful encounter. Smith met him in a local wood and asked to borrow a knife to cut up bread and cheese which she was carrying for her dinner. When she finished, she ran off laughing and waving the knife at him as she ran. He followed her to the brook, took the knife from her and in a rage cut her throat and then began to butcher her. Thorley was always reckoned to be dangerous, if provoked.

There were enough doubts about his intelligence at the trial to set a test to see whether he was sufficiently *compos mentis* to stand trial. Thorley was set to count a score of nails and having succeeded in the task was thought to be a competent candidate for the gallows.

He was hanged at Broughton near Chester by the old fashioned method of driving a cart from under Thorley, leaving him to strangle slowly. It was not until the middle of the next century that the scientific method of hanging, using a weight:height ratio devised by executioner Marwood, was employed. This caused death to be instantaneous.

But this story has one final grim twist. The grotesque horror of the case was compounded by the waggoner who carried the body back to be gibbeted at Congleton. He got drunk and lost the body when it fell out of the cart on his way through Delamere Forest. After a prolonged search the body was found and conveyed to Congleton, where the Reverend Wilson's young charges witnessed the educative experience of seeing Thorley strung up one more time.

A KILLING ON
WETLEY MOOR, 1841

I knew Wetley Moor from childhood. It was not too far from the council estate on which I was brought up. It was especially good in late summer when you could pick bilberries and play commandos amongst the rocks. Cattle would be grazing on the moors and would panic as charging boys forced them to scatter.

I used also to like to take a bird recognition book and an old telescope trying to spot the different birds. Once, I saw a buzzard and nearly stepped on the nest of fledgling skylarks. Do boys from Abbey Hulton still engage in these innocent pleasures on the Moor?

I didn't realise it then, but over 160 years ago Wetley Moor was the scene of a violent death in which my great-great-great-great grandfather, Thomas Sherwin, played a significant part. He was born in 1817 and was part of an extended family that lived in the area for at least 150 years before his birth. His great grandfather, John Sherwin, was born at the beginning of the 18th century. John's remains lie in St Mary's Church in Bucknall. Thomas Sherwin's mother was Susannah Forrester, from another well known local family. In 1838, Thomas married Sarah Hewitt and, at the time that these events took place, had two children, James and Enoch. He was clearly a man of some intelligence and could write his name in a beautiful copperplate hand. As his marriage certificate attests, Thomas Sherwin was a collier. Small mines and coal pits existed around the moor. Mining as an activity had flourished from the middle of the 18th century and reached a peak just after the First World War. When I was a child in the 60s, there was always the fear that there was a mine shaft that could open up on the unwary, whether that be man or beast.

But the focus of the story shifts to the uncle of Thomas Sherwin's wife. William Hewitt was 60 in June 1841 and was a former miner. The newspaper report from the time stated that he lived a mendicant lifestyle. He seemed in a woeful state. The newspaper described him as a 'frugal man and disreputable'. One of the witnesses at the trial said that, shortly before Hewitt's death, the old man was seen carrying a load and looking "clemmed"- a dialect word for starving.

He would have been thought old in the context of the early 19th century, when the expectation of life for working men would have been very low - not much beyond 60. William Hewitt had got into trouble the previous year when he and his brother were imprisoned at Stafford for stealing fowl. He was in jail in October 1840 and released the following spring. The hovel that Hewitt built on the moor had been pulled down and he was homeless. William Hewitt lived by staying at the homes of people who lived on the moor, or by sleeping rough.

He did think of changing his life and at the trial Thomas Sherwin recalled a conversation with Hewitt who told him that he wanted to build a house. He had 16 gold sovereigns and a Mr Perry owed him £22 - enough to build something. Hewitt was a miser although everyone knew that he had money. A farmer called Wilshaw saw a drunken Hewitt drop his money on the road in front of him. His aside is reported in the *Staffordshire Advertiser* in the report of the inquest in June 1841. Wilshaw responded to his neighbour's difficulties with banter: "What, William, are you going to mend the road with sovereigns?"

Wilshaw mentioned this episode to William Simpson, a fellow, according to the newspaper, 'of unprepossessing appearance and intemperate habits'. Simpson liked a pint and a couple days before the death of Hewitt, complained about having no money and that he was looking for work.

Hewitt's body was found at 7am on the 19th June 1841 by a man called Holland. Holland was looking at collecting sand for a house that he was building on the Common. The body had been seen the previous evening by a party of young women walking from Lane End. They thought that the old man was drunk. Holland called on Thomas Sherwin who lived nearby and they established that Hewitt was dead. The body was lying on its back in a stone pit. The left arm was folded across the stomach. His head was resting on a rock. There were two deep head wounds and the body, according to Sherwin, was stiff and cold. The left trouser pocket had been cut off and Hewitt's purse was missing. In the other pocket were one shilling and sixpence and four pence in copper. They called a constable.

A few days afterwards an inquest was held in Hanley, when the details of the death of Hewitt were investigated. I get the impression that the examination of the circumstances that led to the man's death was quite thorough in the short time that was allowed. The surgeon who examined the body determined that Hewitt was beaten with a stone and that his death was not due to a fall.

Constable Allen, the investigating police officer, after a search around the quarry, found a lump of grit stone about five inches across, matted with blood and hair. It was concluded that it was the murder weapon. The cause of death was a fractured skull with two heavy blows to the back of the head. The brain had not been exposed by the attack.

The Magistrate, Job Meigh, made frequent interruptions, especially about the drinking culture at the time. There was a reference to the chief suspect drinking in a pub in Bucknall, the day after the death of the old man - Sunday 20th June. The pub had been opened at 7am, where beer and gin had been drunk for several hours. Meigh did not approve of the "impropriety of disrespecting the Sabbath, by allowing tippling to such an extent on a Sunday" and after giving the landlady of the *Dog and Partridge* a suitable caution, hoped the constable would "strictly do his duty".

The jury returned the verdict of 'wilful killing'. The police already had a suspect in custody - William Simpson had been apprehended by the authorities. Simpson's mother, who gave evidence at the inquest, was hysterical: she recognised that her son faced the prospect, if he was charged with murder, with death by hanging.

Simpson was seen the day of the killing. He lived close by and one witness, Thomas Sherwin's Aunt, Mary Sherwin - a woman in her early 40s - saw Simpson walking in the direction of Armshead from Washerwall at about 2pm, very close to the old man who was warming himself by a clod fire. George Forrester, the uncle of Thomas Sherwin, passed Simpson on a footpath in the direction of the old quarry where earlier he saw Hewitt.

I have seen a map of 1900 of the area. Wetley Moor is about 80 acres in size and rises to above 800 feet in height. It is a leftover of the Gritstone Edge that runs northwards towards Leek into the Pennine Chain. The area is criss-crossed with stone walls and footpaths. There is a great deal of evidence of mining and quarrying in the area, the landscape is dotted with shafts and stone pits. There are three quarries on the map and a footpath that cuts behind a spot called the 'old quarry' and bends towards the trig point of 857 feet and then on to Luzlow and Bagnall.

I am assuming that Hewitt was killed at the site of the old quarries; some distance away from being overlooked by nearby houses.

Simpson's luck changed radically the day after Hewitt's death. He had money and was spending it freely. He redeemed a coat, that he had had in pawn since April, with sovereigns and paid off drinking debts. He 'went up Hanley' where he met his mother and drank liberally in the *New Inn*. He paid off the debt he had run up in that pub by asking what his 'shot' was. He bought a smock frock for eight shillings and in the town met a man called Lunn, an old drinking companion, and offered to loan him a shilling.

The following morning Simpson met with Thomas Sherwin and roused the landlady of the *Dog and Partridge* in Bucknall. The two men stayed there for a few hours, drinking beer and gin. Simpson ate bread and cheese. Sherwin and Simpson parted company and Simpson slept off the effect of the drink in an empty fodder bin. He was found there by Constable Allen.

Simpson was wearing a waistcoat when he was arrested and detained in Hanley. On examination, the Constable noticed a dark stain that could have been blood on the left sleeve and asked Simpson how the garment got to be stained. Simpson claimed that he had a nose bleed in the cell, although there was no evidence of bleeding in the newly changed bed straw.

Simpson was also asked how he came by the money. He replied that he had worked for it and it was money that he got for "bark peeling past Newcastle". Bark peeling was a long-established woodland craft which used the same techniques for centuries. The bark contained a chemical derivative which was used to process animal hides. As proof of his story he produced a receipt, although the constable reported there was a considerable difference between the money that he had received and the recent spending spree.

It looked as if Simpson was doomed. Justice worked very swiftly in the 19th century, and the following month Simpson was on trial for his life at Stafford Assizes. The case was tried by Mr Justice Coltman, an experienced judge who had been trying capital cases for a number of years. Mr Kinnersley and Mr Greaves led for the prosecution while Simpson defended himself. Few working men could afford the costs of a defence lawyer and thus they had to rely on their wits. In the proceedings that were to follow he was to demonstrate some skill in self advocacy. The odds were stacked against them. The prosecution made great play that the evidence was circumstantial, but put strong arguments why they believed that Simpson was guilty.

The names of the people who gave evidence that day and in the other trials are still common in North Staffordshire, names such as Wilshaw, Matthews, Forrester, Bailey, Holland, Mayer, Machin, Leese, Allen, Fallows, Hewitt and Sherwin. The only evidence that seemed to help Simpson was witness inconsistency over the material and ownership of the purse that Simpson had on him at the time of the arrest: there was an inconclusive attempt to link the purse to Hewitt.

All that Simpson said in his defence at the trial is reported in the *Staffordshire Advertiser* of 24th July 1841: "I am innocent of the charge as an unborn child; I have no witness here as I know of".

The Jury took just ten minutes to reach a verdict and found the defendant 'Not guilty'.

There was astonishment in the crowded court; Mr Justice Coltman was unprepared for such a result. I imagine that he was getting ready to don the black cap and pronounce the death penalty. The affair does not end there, however. Simpson went on a heavy drinking bout in the pubs of Stafford on the night of the acquittal and under the influence ranted and raved.

The people who gave evidence against him were a "damned lot of forsworn witnesses all together and when he got home he will make them stand further".

I am assuming that Simpson felt that he had been conspired against and, as the Forresters, Hewitts and Sherwins were all related, had plotted against him.

The speech was heard by Constable Thomas Stone of Bagnall, who warned Simpson that he had a narrow escape and should think himself very well off. Stone warned that if he continued in that way of threatening witnesses then he would find himself in custody.

This did not deter Simpson, who said "Well, I will. I will never kill another man, if I had killed him. If Lunn had gone with me to Kingsley Wakes I should have taken the six sovereigns, and should have hanged and nothing will have saved me".

He was rearrested and a trial date fixed for the following March, when he was to be tried with manslaughter and larceny.

Thomas Sherwin was not a witness at the 1842 trials. On the 31st October 1841, he was killed in a gunpowder explosion in a pit. He died at the pit in Bucknall. The explosion also took the life of a 12 year old boy, Walley. The new mines that grew up in the 19th century depended on men and children working long hours in often dangerous conditions. Accidents were common.

During the 19th century, on average, four miners were killed a day. Thomas Sherwin left a wife and two small boys. The children would not have known their father. Sarah Sherwin remarried Charles Wilshaw in 1853.

The following spring, Simpson faced the lesser crimes of manslaughter and robbery. The trial was played out again with little new evidence. The newspaper reported that Simpson questioned the witnesses on the subject of the colour and material of the purse that Hewitt had with considerable shrewdness.

For a second time, Simpson was found not guilty while admitting that he had taken the purse from Hewitt's corpse. The third trial was a formality and was over in minutes; Simpson was found guilty and transported to Australia for seven years.

The Judge at the trial, in passing sentence, made the following remark: "It would ill become me, now that you are convicted of this offence, to comment on the degree of guilt in which you have been involved in the same transaction; this is a matter between you and God."

Transportation of convicts to Australia started in 1787. By 1840, transportation to New South Wales had ceased, but it continued to Tasmania and Western Australia until 1853. Prisoners who received a transportation sentence were not normally allowed to return to the UK. It is estimated that between 1789-1870, over 150,000 Britons forcibly colonised Australia in this way.

Most prisoners receiving a transportation sentence were sent initially to the Prison Hulks in London and served the first part of their sentence in solitary confinement, before being assigned to a convict ship and leaving England.

In one sense, Simpson was fortunate to get a sentence of seven years: at the same Assize, a man from Penn, near Wolverhampton, was sentenced to ten years for stealing a sheep.

Given the evidence, how would modern forensic detection have worked? Fingerprint evidence was not introduced until 1900 and DNA was first used in 1986. I imagine that today, work would have been done on the blood on the sleeve of Simpson's waistcoat. The purse would have been examined to see if it contained material linking it to Hewitt. A pathologist would be able to ascertain how and when Hewitt met his death, and how the fateful wounds were delivered. Evidence would have been taken over time to try to link Simpson and Hewitt.

This piece began with a death and ends with a death. Thomas Sherwin was not the first or last Sherwin to die as a consequence of mining. Over 40 years after the death of Thomas, three other Sherwins went underground to die. In October 1889, fire damp at the Mossfield Colliery near Longton took the lives of 64 miners. Three of the miners were Thomas, Charles and Samuel Sherwin. Sam was just 16. The father, William, was also a miner and never went down the pit again. With the compensation from the mining company the father and mother opened a bakery in Werrington. A story has it that a pair of clogs belonging to one of the young men was hung over the grave in Caverswall Graveyard.

CHILDREN'S STREET SONGS

My daughter taught me a clapping game from the school playground that goes "Teacher, teacher over there, what colour is your underwear, is it black or is it white? O my gosh it's dynamite. 9,8,7,6 5,4,3,2,1. Schools out". There is another one she sings which is rather rude about school dinners and their purging effect: "I feel sick, toilet quick".

This is of course not a new tradition. It goes back a long way and is certainly international, with songs and games collected globally. My mother in her 80s told me of the song that they sung in Stoke about Mrs Simpson and the Abdication crisis "She's been married twice before and now she's knocking on Eddy's door". Or north country children on the grisly Dr Ruxton murders of 1936 "Red stains on the carpet, red stains on the knife, Oh Dr Ruxton, You've murdered your wife". They can be topical as well as subversive.

The subject has fascinated folklorists for a long time. It's over 50 years since the husband and wife team, the

Opies, chronicled the play and street songs of children in Britain. They attempted to counter the notion that in an age of television the tradition had died. They also suggested that new songs could be passed on very quickly. The Opies proved the custom was still alive. I recall as a kid growing up in Stoke parodying Beatles' songs "Is there anything that you want?" "Fish and Chips" would be the shouted reply. It's good to see that the tradition still continues.

It is something that changes with the times and is thriving. Only last summer I saw a group of children near the *Wellington* pub in Leek act out a version of the *X Factor*. Another group of children was judging a small girl on her singing ability. One of the children said, "I'll be Simon". The girl won through.

I can happily conclude that, even with the demands on children's time, the street songs and games still have power to poke fun at figures of authority and have relevance.

THE CIRCUS
COMES TO TOWN

In October 1925, a wonderfully evocative letter was published in the *Leek Times*. A poster of a forthcoming event in the market had triggered distant memories of an event burned into the writer's mind. Bostock and Wombwell Menagerie was hitting town and notices were on the hoardings.

The Circus was coming, re-visiting a town with which they had strong connections. When Bostock and Wombwell Menagerie came to town it was opening the casket of memory for one elderly resident who felt compelled to write to the paper, chronicling a visit made by the circus to the Leek of his boyhood.
.

'I can still remember the old show 60 years ago', the letter from 'Old Resident' began. 'I had the pleasure of visiting the show as a child of ten. It was a gala day ... everyone waited patiently for the advance guard of tiny coloured ponies to arrive ... The memory revives such happy memories. The great day arrived and we did not want any calling. Most of the town was up at an early hour, forming a procession as the menagerie entered the town. The wagons, some pulled by horses, harness all shining, others drawn by elephants and camels, came into view. What a shout went up when we saw the first wagon. All of us eager to ride in the manager's trap, pointing out the best way to the showground. The canvas canopies were soon fixed up in the market place. The crowd would be harangued with stories of how dangerous the animals were and the public were begged to look for themselves. The lion tamer was dressed in a red jacket with gold braiding and wearing many medals. He was our hero and our ambition was to be a lion hunter, nothing else was sufficiently dangerous when we grew up.

'The Band - and what a good band they were - at the front all dressed in top hats and frock coats. The show had opened and my father carried me on his shoulders. I saw the first wild animals I had ever seen: it was an education. What a pleasant recollection the old show brings to my mind! What happy carefree boyhood days!'

'Old Resident' then went on to mention the family connection between the Bostock's and the area. The original partner in the business, James Bostock, had been born in 1815 at the Dairy House, Horton and joined Wombwell's Menagerie in 1830 as a Waggoner and a trainer of horses, a skill he acquired on the family farm. He acted as advance agent for 28 years for the company — the high points being when he presented the menagerie before the royal family in 1847 and 1854 at Windsor Castle. He died in 1878 in Surrey. One of the Bostocks had run a grocery in Church Street and a relative Frank Bostock lived in Alsop Street.

James Bostock's son, Edward Bostock, wrote a very entertaining book called *Menageries, Circus and*

Theatres in 1927, which details the family connections between Bostocks in Leek and the family business. There is a section on how he met his wife after suffering an occupational hazard. Following an attack by a hyena at a show in Stockport, Edward recuperated in Leek and was nursed back by his wife to be Elizabeth. They married at St Edward's Church in Leek in August 1881.

The account is a marvellous depiction of life at the edges in Victorian Britain. His autobiography has so many stories that there is enough material to make a very interesting book or film. There are instances when animals got out and wandered amongst the audience. As a boy on tour with the menagerie in Ireland, he saw a stampede when a lion got into a crowd, as well as extremely risky acts such as a tiger mounted on the back of an elephant riding around the auditorium in Glasgow in 1892.

He demonstrated the excitement that people in rural communities must have felt and which comes through in Old Resident's letter as the menagerie came into town. Edward uses the expression 'Booming the show' to describe the procession. At the front were the bandsman well-dressed and playing the popular tunes of the time. Sometimes the circus would arrive at evening and their way would be lighted by naphtha flares. Fires seemed to be a common occurrence and several are detailed in the book. Derring-do acts of bravery are also frequently carried out as Edward and others rescue the animals at one event at the Goose Fair in Nottingham, when the canvas catches fire. In 1872 in Hanley an elephant trampled to death a 14 year old boy. It is a terrible event, but no blame is attached to the animal as it seems that the boy was provoking it. There does not seem to be much regard for health and safety. Early in his career Bostock went into a lion cage with a trainer who had had too much to drink and, towards the end, he rescued a drunken trapeze artist who was tangled up in ropes many feet above the ground.

The journeys that the menagerie made were truly heroic. In the winter of 1875, they walked through a blizzard over the Yorkshire Wolds. The horses were rough shod, as the roads were sheets of ice. The wagons were skidding down the hills and they had no control as cages containing lions and tigers and bears slithered into ditches. By the time they get to Sheriff Hutton at night, the racoons have escaped and in the dark are difficult to find. The team had to crawl on their hands and knees in the snow to find the animals. The wagon containing the wolves was lost and, by the time it arrived the following day, the wolves were fine but the Wagoner, known as the Dodger, was so cold that he had frozen to the seat and had to be thawed out before an open fire and generous amounts of brandy poured down his throat before he was revived.

But what conditions must the animals have had to put up with. The animals must have suffered terribly cramped conditions as well as the great extremes of the British climate. The constant journeying must have been trying for animals and people. Edward detailed a tour they took in 1883/4 when he visited Burton on Trent, Tutbury Ashbourne, Derby, Nottingham Sunderland, Galashiels, Edinburgh, Stirling, Perth, Dunkeld, Pitlochry, Kingussie, Inverness, Wick, Thurso, Foress, Aberdeen, Forfar, Fife, Edinburgh, Glasgow, York, Hull, Beverley, Filey and Scarborough.

One story that is told predates Edward Bostock's

involvement with the menagerie and is an indicator of the cruelty of the menagerie in the very early days. It is also an excellent reflection on the idiocy of mankind. Edward records that Wombwell in 1825 wanted to recreate the *Circus Maximus* of Ancient Rome. He decided to use mastiff dogs to attack a lion. A large crowd had gathered at the event in Liverpool, but the dogs were so cowed and the lion so docile that nothing happened. The enraged crowd, which had been drinking heavily, turned on each other while the animals passively watched the rioting humans.

Bostock and Wombwell finally wound up in 1931 in recognition of the part the town had played in the history of the company Leek was included in the final tour. The animals formed the core of the collection of the newly opened Whipsnade Zoo.

THE FORGERS OF BOTTOMHOUSE INN, 1801

This fascinating account of a team of forgers operating in the Staffs Moorlands in the early years of the 1800s was unearthed through the pages of the *Staffordshire Advertiser*, which I found in the William Salt Library in Stafford.

The Bottomhouse Inn was in existence in the 18th century and run by George Fearns, who was part of an extended family that lived in the Bottomhouse and Ipstones area. Counterfeiting was a serious business in the early years of the 19th century and the authorities took any attempt to debase the currency very seriously. Being caught with an amount of counterfeit notes could lead to the death penalty being imposed. The Bank of England was aware that forgers were at work around Leek and, following information from an arrest at Congleton, dispatched Joseph Nadin, a leading thief-taker from Manchester, to find out who was behind the law-breaking.

The *Staffordshire Advertiser* of August 1801 gave a full account of the circumstances that lead to the arrest of George Fearns. Nadin took the assumed name William Rivers and was accompanied by another Manchester constable, Marshall Knowles. They assumed the disguise of peddlers and stopped at the inn with calico and hessian cloth. They attempted to lull Fearns into a false sense of security and gradually they won over his confidence. Nadin told Fearns that the times were hard and it was difficult for an honest man to make a living. Later they took rum and milk. Nadin found fault with the rum and told the landlord that he could get better from Manchester. Fearns joked that he did not take Nadin for a smuggler. Nadin told him the price which he could have the cheap rum by avoiding excise. The Manchester man said that he had the rum covered with American flour and hidden under cloth.

Fearns admired Nadin's nerve. He also told him that the hessian was "swag", too, and put down a forged guinea note taken in a case in Chester. Marshall rather bluntly asked Fearns whether he had any "screeves" or counterfeit notes and, as the conversation turned, the attitude of Fearns changed: he became, to use a dialect word of the time, 'licksome'. Nadin asked about another local criminal that he claimed to know called Jackson. Fearns said that he had "gone out of the country" - in other words, transported for cattle rustling. The constables asked the landlord's opinion about a number of dodgy notes they had, leading Fearns on. Today we would call this entrapment. Nadin said that he intended to "smash" them or put them into circulation in Congleton. He had spent one a few days earlier at the Bull in Congleton.

Fearns said that it was a wonder that they were not "legged" or caught and "that a man had been taken there and was now at Chester Gaol and he had snitched about me". As a result the Yeomanry from Leek had searched the area. Fearns went away and showed the two men a variety of notes he had got from a forger based in Walsall. He threw him a five guinea screeve that he had bought for one and a half guineas. He was going into Yorkshire soon to "smash" some notes there. Fearns told Nadin how to age the notes by rubbing them with a sweaty hand in one way and to not 'squeeze' the watermark, to make them look right.

Fearns said that he and his brother Tom had, "gone into Wales and also to Chester Fair and we smashed them about £500 of them by buying cattle and horses, which I took into Nottinghamshire and sold them. I have a licence to deal in horses". Nadin continued the probing questions and asked Fearns whether he knew Long Tom Morley. Fearns did not know his surname but he came to Bottomhouse once a month and he brought many screeves with him. Marshall, who had left earlier on a pretext, arrived with the Constables and Fearns was taken into custody. He was imprisoned at Stafford and hanged in August 1801.

The case has an interesting postscript. In July 1817 Sarah Wardle, a 34 year old woman married with three children, was convicted of having a counterfeit £1 on her. She was sentenced for 14 years' transportation. Sarah, who was born in Ipstones in 1777, was described as "being of middling stature with dark grey eyes and brown hair inclined to sandy". She was dressed like a 'decent serving girl'. However, on 11th January 1818, she managed to escape from Stafford Jail. It later transpired that she had bribed the guards with money that her 13 year old daughter had brought into the jail. The ease with which she did this lead me to think that she was aided by an organisation and that lead me to think that a counterfeit gang was continuing in operation some time after the demise of George Fearns.

And, intriguingly... were Sarah and George related?

GEORGE ELIOT AND STAFFORDSHIRE

Warwickshire has acclaim as the home of Mary Ann Evans, better known to posterity as George Eliot. She took a male name because she remained very sensitive to criticism. She was anxious to avoid being patronised as a woman writer and followed the example of the Brontes in using a male pseudonym.

Her family roots, however, lie in Warwickshire and, particularly, in Nuneaton, her birthplace, as well as in Coventry, which had a strong impact on her early development. However, it is Ellastone on the borders of Staffordshire and Derbyshire which proved the inspiration for her first novel, *Adam Bede*, published in 1859. The village and the association with someone who has a very strong claim as Britain's first modern novelist, has proved popular with the tourist board which is strongly promoting the link. Ellastone is beautifully situated under the brow of the Weaver Hills and the attractiveness of the countryside captivated the novelist, who gave the name of Hayslope to Ellastone:

'The rich undulating district of Loamshire (Staffordshire) to which Hayslope belonged lies close to the grim outskirts of Stoneyshire (Derbyshire) overlooked by barren hills as a pretty blooming sister may sometimes be seen linked in the arm of a rugged, tall, swarthy brother; and in two hours ride the traveller might exchange a bleak treeless region, intersected by lines of cold grey stone, for one where his road wound under the shelter of woods, or up swelling hills, muffled with hedgerows and long-meadow grass and thick corn; and where at every turn he came past fine old country seats nestled in the valley or crowning the slope.'

Adam Bede is a country novel which chronicles the lives of villagers in the North Midlands at the beginning of the 19th century, a way of life which would rapidly disappear. The principal character, Bede, is a carpenter based on Eliot's own father, a highly principled individual who is in love with Hetty Sorrel, the high spirited niece of Farmer Poyser. She is seduced by the young squire and becomes pregnant. The young woman is abandoned and hurriedly leaves the area. Hetty is later charged with the murder of the child. The young Methodist preacher, Dinah Morris, spends a great deal of time at Hetty's side as she is convicted and sentenced to death. Hetty is reprieved and transported to Australia while Adam forges a new relationship with Dinah.

The central figure, the carpenter who, as previously stated, is based on Robert Evans, the father of the novelist, who had a strong sense of honour and work ethic. He remained an unwavering Tory throughout his life and his strong personality would later clash with her equally strong-willed daughter. She was full of admiration for him,

'He had a large knowledge of building, of mines, of plantations, of various branches of valuation and measurement, of all that is essential to the management of large estates.'

She clearly showed an interest in his work, as the scene in the carpenters shop was always admired as being an accurate portrayal of the profession. The central theme of the novel, the fate of Hetty, was a result of a conversation that Eliot had with her Aunt Elizabeth Tomlinson. She was a Methodist preacher, who befriended a young woman, Mary Voce, who murdered her illegitimate child and was hanged in Nottingham in 1804.

The fate of young working class women who bore children out of wedlock was frequently a grim one as they faced the opprobrium of a moralising society.

The judgement of society is something that women who found themselves in this situation continued to face throughout the 19th century. In the decade of Eliot's death in 1886 there is a report in a local paper of a young woman in Sheen, Mary Lomas, a domestic servant, who died after an attempt to conceal a pregnancy. Neither mother nor child survived. Earlier in the century in 1859, Sarah Middleton of Flash, died in a field in an advanced state of pregnancy. The voice of the working class woman suffering from poverty is rarely heard, but occasionally it comes through.

There exists an unusual archive of a series of letters written by Ellen Parker, born in 1790 in Alton, a pauper who wrote to the authorities in Stafford as she was bringing up a number of children following the death of her husband. The response of authority was at first caring, but when she became pregnant with a sixth child following a brief relationship, the attitude to her shifted. She moved from the category of deserving poor into the category of undeserving. The pressure and obloquy that women who were in this situation faced caused some to resort to desperate measures as was the case with Voce.

Elizabeth Tomlinson appears from biographies of Eliot to be a saintly woman who preached throughout Staffordshire and Derbyshire and it is thought that she preached in the open air on the Green at Ellastone. Her fame travelled far and Queen Victoria had a picture of Tomlinson wearing a distinctive Quaker bonnet.

Many of Eliot's family lie buried in the area. Her grandparents lie in Norbury Church over the River Dove. The church is said to contain examples of woodwork by Robert Evans who learnt his trade in the area. She was taken to the area on several occasions by her father and a lengthy visit happened in 1839/40 where she gathered information which she used in her book some 20 years later. A letter published in an 1888 biography of Eliot sets out a journey that Eliot made in 1839 when she was staying with her Staffordshire relatives.

'Ashbourne Church, the finest mere parish church in the kingdom - in the interior; of Alton Gardens where I saw actually what I had often seen mentally - the bread fruit - in the interior; of the fan palm and the papyrus; and of last Lichfield cathedral.'

In the novel Eliot also uses local names such as Poyser a number of whom still appear in the Staffs Moorlands telephone directory. She describes with a great deal of detail the lives of the peasantry, knowing that the country in the period that the novel was set was poised on the brink of great change.

'Those old women scraping carrots with their work worn hands, those heavy clowns taking holiday in a dingy pot house, those round backs and stupid weather-beaten faces that have bent over a spade and done the rough work of the world - those homes with their tin pans, their brown pitchers, their rough curs, and their cluster of onions.'

At one point in the narrative, even oatcakes are mentioned.

When she published the novel she was criticised for including the dialect of Staffordshire and it was suggested that she change it, along with the controversial scene of Hetty giving birth in a field. Her response was terse.

'I would rather have my teeth drawn than part with either.'

She also alters the names of local place names in the book, so that The Weaver Hills become the Binton Hills, Eagledale is Dovedale, Oakthorpe becomes Ashbourne and Wotton Park is Donnithorne Chase. Local characters also appear in the novel: a well-remembered and loved Vicar, George Hake, becomes Aldophous Irwine.

The book was published in 1859 and was well received right from the beginning; the writer Charles Reade called it the 'finest thing since Shakespeare'. Charles Dickens was equally enthusiastic: '*Adam Bede* has taken its place among the actual experiences of my life.' In Russia, Tolstoy approved of the novel. 1859 was a bumper year as far as publications of ground breaking books was concerned. Apart from *Adam Bede*, it was the year of the publication of John Stuart Mills *On Liberty* and another book with strong Staffordshire connections, Charles Darwin's *The Origin of Species*. Eliot had a keen interest in the natural sciences and was aware that the old certainties of faith were under strain, an assertion that is reflected in her work, especially in her first novel.

But in *Adam Bede,* Eliot portrayed men and women in their struggles and sufferings. The characters are rooted in a time and in a place in Staffordshire which provided the background to one of the finest novels of the Victorian period.

HAROLD DAVIES MP GOES TO VIETNAM, 1965

It is a very rare occasion that the activities of the MP for Leek would feature as a question at a US Presidential press conference, but it did happen. The President was Lyndon Johnson and the extraordinary incident was a secret peace mission to North Vietnam undertaken by Harold Davies at the behest of Labour Prime Minister, Harold Wilson, in July 1965.

But first a little explanation is required. Davies, a fiery, left-wing MP from South Wales, was first elected to the Leek constituency in the Labour Party landslide of 1945.

He was a very assiduous MP, proved by the incredible hard work he put into his constituency, which at the time included a part of what is now Stoke on Trent. Reading the newspapers from the 1950s and 60s it seems that Davies was everywhere. He was involved in rural issues, especially the supply of water to the remote parts of the constituency. He helped secure the main office site for the Britannia Building Society, and took a keen interest in comprehensive education. He was an ardent supporter of public housing in areas of the constituency such as Weston Coyney as well as keeping the *Leek Post and Times* regularly supplied with copy of his parliamentary exploits. He was a regular contributor in debates. It seems he had to be, as his parliamentary majority in the 50s barely rose above 1,000 votes.

Davies was also well-connected and, during the 50s, a stream of important Labour Party figures spoke in the constituency, including future Labour party leaders Jim Callaghan and Michael Foot. But perhaps the greatest coup was during the 1955 General Election when the great hero of the left, the creator of the NHS and fellow Welshman, Aneurin Bevan, spoke at Kidsgrove Town Hall.

However, one thing is certain, Davies was an expert on South East Asia and he wrote frequently on the subject, often in learned journals, which were carried faithfully by the Post and Times.

Davies wrote critically of American action in Korea especially the gung ho tactics of the American general McArthur during the early 50s. The Leek MP visited Moscow in 1952, commenting that he had previously visited the Soviet Union capital in 1938 when he was a WEA Lecturer. He was remarkably uncritical of life in Moscow in what was the last year of the tyrannical rule of Stalin. Davies wrote about the happy citizenry when the reality for many Soviet people was terror, repression and the Gulags. Many on the left were, it seems, blind to the cruelties of the Communist system.

In 1955 Davies undertook a long and difficult trip to Mao's China, writing regular articles to the *Post and*

Times on what he found in the People's Republic:

'China is not a side-show in world affairs. She is a living and powerful reality. The West must adjust itself to the regime of Mao Tse Tung and it is here to stay.'

He visited farms, factories and mines in China and praised the economic development in the country, barely a decade from the time when the Communists had taken power.

'The miners would have been at home in the North Staffs Coalfield. The seam I saw was at an angle of 45 degrees and some six feet in height was being cut at a time. I crawled for some 30 yards to the main conveyer belt and followed it to the main loading belt where a Russian diesel engine puffed along, pulling some 20 or more trams to the pit bottom... This is China, the old and the new tumbling incongruously into the lap of history'.

In 1959 Davies was on his travels again to the Philippines and Vietnam, when he met the leader of the North Vietnamese Communist Party, Ho Chi Minh. Ho had fought in campaigns firstly against the Japanese during the Second World War and in the early 50s against the French. The French colonialists were beaten and the country became involved in a civil war between the Communist North and the non-Communist South. 1959 involved North Vietnamese in insurgency actions in the South.

To his credit, Davies at an early stage did not believe in the prevailing military doctrine espoused by elements of the American Government, that Vietnam was another piece in the falling dominoes following China and Korea and that the country was rife for a communist take over. Davies believed, and history has proved him correct in this analysis, that Vietnam was a civil war.

By the early 60s, it was clear that Britain would soon face political change. Under its new leader, Harold Wilson, a Labour Government was returned at the 1964 General Election, but with a majority of just four it was not in a strong position. The new Prime Minister had to appease the left wing of the Labour party, represented by people like Harold Davies and there was also the problem of the Americans. The US President in this period was a no-nonsense, bluff Texan, Lyndon Johnson, who had succeeded the assassinated Kennedy in 1963. Johnson was convinced of the need to escalate the war in Vietnam and wanted to involve British troops. Wilson pointed out to the President that Britain was doing its bit fighting Communist rebels in Malaysia.

This did not wear with the President and Wilson conceived of the idea of a secret peace mission to involve a man who was known to have a keen interest in the region. He asked Davies to go to Vietnam.

In July 1965, Davies was prepared to take the long trip to South East Asia. The hope was that Davies would be allowed a visa to visit Hanoi and be able to see the senior political figures in the North Vietnamese capital. However it was important that the trip was kept secret from both the British and Vietnamese perspective. According to Wilson, the details of the visit were disastrously leaked to the British press. By the time the Leek MP got to Hanoi there was bitter recrimination and Davies was ostracised, seeing only minor officials and having no meeting with Ho Chi Minh.

The Americans were highly critical of the visit and had no confidence in the Welshman. They were concerned that Davies was travelling on his own, did not have diplomatic experience, did not speak French, was a talkative left wing sympathiser and 'is not noted for his judgement'.

Some British Foreign Office officials agreed with the judgement of the Americans and the British Ambassador to the US, David Bruce, believed that Harold Davies was a person who 'could be easily used by the communists' and that the Prime Minister should never have supported the proposal. One of the Labour Cabinet Ministers, Richard Crossman, damned the initiative as a gimmick. Another, Barbara Castle, was aware that Harold Wilson feared the press leak undermined the secrecy of the visit, but was 'well satisfied with the gesture.' mainly because it put some distance between the British and the Americans. The central problem was that neither the Vietnamese nor the Americans were in the game of going down a path of a negotiated settlement. The Hawks outnumbered the Doves and both were committed to escalating the war. President Johnson still felt that there was something to gain by building up American military involvement in South East Asia. News came from the White House that further British initiatives such as the Davies trip would do more harm than good because it undermined the American position and gave an impression to the Communists that the Americans were suing for peace.

Back in Leek. the *Post and Times* carried a small article headlined 'Leek MP hits world headlines with visit to war torn Vietnam'. The article mentioned the visit in the briefest of details.

The Vietnam War, of course, dragged on throughout the 60s and is regarded as part of the iconography of the decade. It effectively wrecked the political career of President Johnson and ended with the South Vietnamese capital Saigon falling to Viet Cong forces in 1975. Many millions of Vietnamese were killed, as were 60,000 Americans, and it has taken some time to recover. Harold Davies finally lost the Leek seat following boundary changes in 1970 and went to the House of Lords as Lord Davies of Leek.

ADMIRAL GAUNT— 'JAMES BOND'?

I came across the name of Admiral Sir Guy Gaunt whilst researching a piece on Baden-Powell, the founder of the Scout Movement, who visited Leek in the summer of 1920. Sir Guy was part of the welcoming party that accompanied the hero of Mafeking as he visited Scout troops, eventually staying with Sir Guy and his wife at their home, Swainsley Hall, in the Manifold Valley.

Entirely in character, Baden-Powell spent the night under canvas in the grounds of Swainsley Hall, much to the amusement of his hosts. Sir Guy's wife was Margaret Worthington, daughter of Thomas Wardle, the Leek industrialist. Thomas Wardle had owned

Swainsley, the house passing into his daughter's ownership in 1909 after his death.

I thought that I would find out a little more about Gaunt. He sounded intriguing.

He was born in Australia in 1869. He attended Melbourne Grammar School and, despite a parental desire that he go into law, had a yearning for the sea, eventually joining a training ship for Merchant Navy officers. He soon transferred to the Royal Navy where his dashing, reckless manner bought him to a wider public. In 1897, while serving on *HMS Porpoise*, he came to the defence of the British Consulate at Samoa, repelling a rebel attack. In following uprisings he raised and led a native force that became known as 'Gaunt's Brigade', earning him a Mention in Despatches and rapid promotion. He was a natural leader, extremely able, a formidable linguist - he spoke several languages - ruthless and a very good shot. Gaunt was also debonair, dashing and something of a ladies man.

His commands included ultimately the battleship *HMS Thunderer*. With a scintillating career as naval officer established, he seemed the ideal candidate to become the naval attaché to the United States, an appointment he took up in June 1914, just as the First World War was about to break out.

It proved an ideal appointment as he was able to demonstrate to his superiors his drive and adaptability in a situation that was vital to the successful prosecution of the war. He was fully engaged in intelligence work, countering the activities of secret agents and saboteurs from enemy powers. He worked closely with various nationalist groups such as the Czechs, looking to form their own country in the aftermath of the war.

Gaunt successfully infiltrated the Hindu-German conspiracy that attempted to ferment rebellion in British India and was involved in the British machinations surrounding the infamous Zimmerman telegram that drew the US into the war. Gaunt captured one high profile German saboteur and killed or captured a number of other enemy spies. He also helped to run the spy network set up by Balkan nationalists in major American cities and disrupted German intelligence efforts to such good effect that he was the automatic choice to become the senior liaison officer to the USA when President Wilson reluctantly declared war in 1917.

In 1918, with the United States now firmly on the Allied side, American intelligence officers took over responsibilities that he had handled so effectively and Gaunt's request to go back to sea was granted by the Admiralty. However, he was soon appointed to the naval intelligence staff in London and promoted to Rear Admiral, where he worked on the Bolshevik threat. He retired from the Navy at the end of the war with the final rank of Admiral and was awarded a knighthood for services rendered to the State. It was at this stage that he settled in the Staffordshire Moorlands, standing unsuccessfully in the 1918 General Election in Leek for the Tories. He did eventually become an MP for an East Yorkshire constituency, before being forced to resign having been named as a co-respondent in a divorce case in 1926.

While over 70 years of age when World War Two broke out, he remained active and there are records of correspondence between him and naval intelligence officers. It is highly likely that the young intelligence officers of the Second World War would have sought his advice and used his knowledge. They would have known of him without a doubt, because his exploits in the war barely 20 years before were legendary in the cloudy world of naval intelligence: even if the general public only knew of him as an old sea dog with an eye for the women. He died in 1953.

Fans have debated who might have been the model for Ian Fleming's most famous creation the fictitious secret agent James Bond. A number of names have been suggested that make up the personality of the super agent and perhaps the character is a composite of a number of people.

Gaunt has been regarded as a possible prospect by some authorities. He was handsome, suave, brilliantly effective, well-connected, remorseless, an expert shot, multilingual, served as an officer in the Royal Navy and, at the time of his intelligence activities during the First World War, held the substantive rank of Commander, just like the fictitious Bond. His other qualification for the part was proved later in life when he was cited in a notorious divorce case that resulted in the failure of his own marriage. He later married a woman many years his junior with whom he had two daughters. Is it possible that 'James Bond' lived in the Moorlands?

'A FIERY SWORD', 1680

In the parish records at Alstonefield is recorded an astrological phenomenon witnessed by the villagers: 'Very strange and fiery meteors in form like a sword, appeared North West by west in December 1680, and continued about six weeks after which ensued a long and tedious drought.'

Between 1663 and 1680 there were five comets seen over England which to the contemporary mind linked celestial activities and the unsettled times that the country was living through with plague, pestilence and revolution all occurring at this time. There is a sense that whoever wrote the comments in the parish journal was simply echoing the feelings of the time that comets seen in the sky were a fearful celestial sign of events that were being played out on earth. People all over the world believed that the Day of Judgement was approaching.

But the 17th century saw a growing interest in the heavens through the work of Galileo, Newton and Halley, aided by technological advances such as telescopes and an intellectual framework on which to develop concepts

On 14th November 1680, Gottfried Kirch the German astronomer, detected a new comet, becoming on that day the first person to discover a comet using a telescope. Astronomers throughout Europe tracked its position for several months. It was visible in the Northern hemisphere and by the end of that year the comet became bright enough to be seen at noon as it completed its hairpin turn around the Sun. The long, golden tail of the comet of 1680 was estimated to be 30 million miles in length.

Originally thought to be two comets, the comets of late 1680 and early 1681 were in fact a single comet observed before and after perihelion - the point closest to the sun - a situation that hindsight reveals as critical in the determination of the comet's trajectory. Upon examining the course of comets, it is easy to believe that some of them must occasionally fall into the sun. The comet of 1680 approached so near, that, at its perihelion, it was not more distant from the sun than a sixteenth part of its diameter; and if, as some predict, it returns in the year 2255, it may then fall into the sun. This must depend upon the accidents it meets with in its course, and the retardation it suffers in passing through the sun's atmosphere.

MAJOR OLCOTT AND MADAM BLAVATSKY, 1889

The American, Colonel Henry Olcott, is the only speaker at the Nicholson Institute, as far as I am aware, ever to have a national day proclaimed after him, as well as appearing on a national stamp. Olcott spoke at the Institute in November 1889, as the guest of Ralph de Sneyd Tunstall of Onecote - mystic, collector and eccentric. Both were involved in the Theosophical Society founded in New York by Madame Blavatsky.

The Society developed in response to the interest shown in the Victorian period in spiritualism and Eastern religions. Sneyd, who was fascinated with the occult, met Blavatsky in 1889. He fell under the spell of the movement and arranged for Olcott, later to become President of the Society, to give a talk in Leek.

Olcott was a very interesting man. He was the only Yankee journalist to attend the execution of John Brown in 1859 after the failed uprising at Harper's Ferry - one of the causes of the American Civil War.

He was also a member of the Board of Inquiry set up after the assassination of President Lincoln. He later moved to Ceylon, or Sri Lanka as it is now known, and was one of the instigators of the Buddhist Nationalist revival which fuelled the independence movement. He is commemorated on a Sri Lankan stamp and the date of his death, 19th February, is honoured by the lighting of candles.

Sri Lanka is in the news now. There are substantial accusations of war crimes carried out by the army following the ending of a particularly bloody civil war involving the separatist Tamil Tigers, who also committed atrocities. Over 40,000 civilians, many of them children, died in the final stages and the covering up of these events has caused international condemnation. They are not brought to book because they have powerful friends in India. The Indians don't want to upset the Sri Lankans as their business interests are threatened — in the same way that the Russians excuse the behaviour of the Syrians and the West overlook the Chinese actions in Tibet. Sadly, commercial interests will always trump human rights every time and the result is that innocents suffer.

'TELLING MANY A TALE' - THE CRIMEAN WAR, 1855

The *Staffordshire Advertiser* of 30th January 1855 carried in its pages a series of fascinating letters from a young Leek man fighting in the Crimean war written to his brother in England. The documents offer an absorbing insight into a war that is remembered in such phrases as 'the thin red line' and 'Charge of the Light Brigade'.

The charge involved Sergeant Major John Allen, later the landlord of *The Swan* in Leek. The Leek correspondent was a private soldier in the 20th Regiment of Foot, later the Lancashire Fusiliers. He and Allen were part of an allied force fighting the Russian Empire.

How did we find ourselves in a war against the Russians? The cause of the war was a fear that Czarist Russia was looking at expanding its territory at the expense of a disintegrating Ottoman Empire. The British and French felt that such a growth threatened their own colonial interests and war was declared in 1854.

The condition of the British Army was poor. Officers bought their commissions. The ordinary soldiers were of poor quality and discipline was enforced by flogging. (The Leek soldier, however seems to have been pious and conscientious). The leadership was also lamentable. The Commander in Chief was the elderly Lord Raglan who had lost an arm at Waterloo nearly 40 years before. He frequently had to be reminded that the French were no longer the enemy. It should be said that the French were the more professional army as they had seen recent conflict in Algeria.

Our soldier left England on the *Columba* on 17th July 1854. It was an eventful voyage: there was a collision with a Portuguese vessel in the Bay of Biscay. The 20th regiment had a brief stay in Malta and they were later caught in a dreadful storm in the Mediterranean. The battered convoy arrived in Constantinople on 1st August. They reached the Crimea weeks later. It was an impressive force. There were 400 ships in the flotilla. The travel-weary soldier started on the march to Sevastapol on 19th September and marched 40 miles. The force comprised of 80,000 French and British troops. Sevastopol was the main port and was surrounded by hills. He was soon in action. His regiment assaulted the heights above the town with heavy losses: 'it was a dreadful sight to see', he commented. The British marched on to Black River where again they were brought up in battle array, but the Russians retreated.

The 20th Regiment of Foot became involved in one of the major battles of the campaign, at Inkerman, when they were part of the Second Division under the command of Sir George Cathcart. The Regiment was stationed at Shell Hill above Sevastapol. The

Russians launched an attack on the heights in the early hours of 5th November, which nearly took the British by surprise. It was a bloody and closely fought affair, as a report from the *New York Times* describes: 'It was a series of dreadful deeds of daring, of sanguinary hand-to-hand fights, of despairing rallies, of desperate assaults - in glens and valleys, in brushwood glades and remote dells, hidden from all human eyes. No one, however placed, could have witnessed even a small portion of the doings of this eventful day; for the vapours, fog and drizzling mist, obscured the ground where the struggle took place to such an extent as to render it impossible to see what was going on at the distance of a few yards'.

The Leek soldier was heavily involved in the heavy fighting which took the life, among the 597 British soldiers that Sunday morning, of Commander Cathcart. The soldier was forlorn: 'I have left many thousands of my brother soldiers dead on the field of battle, praying that their souls are in heaven in a far better place than where any are of us are at this time. The miseries that I endure are unaccountable'.

He was cold and starving as there were difficulties with transporting supplies, handicapped by impassable roads and frequent blizzards. Basic supplies were not getting through. The French, by contrast, had better stores. Stuck in the trenches before Sevastapol, he was knee deep in mud and water. The conditions predict those endured by First World War soldiers 60 years later. 'May God send you and yours may not suffer what I have suffered', he wearily wrote. He sent his brother a gift of three red feathers taken from the hat of a Russian General at Inkerman. He asked that they be distributed to friends and his niece Ann: 'I could tell you things that would blood turn chilly, if I should return I could tell you many a tale'. The ink with which the soldier had written his letter was made from gunpowder, as there was a shortage of ink and paper.

The fate of the Leek soldier is unknown, but his account indicates that the lot of the ordinary soldier is a common one throughout the ages.

SIR BERTRAM
AND THE WOLF

It took 100 years for Christianity to establish itself in England after Augustine landed in Kent in 597. It seems that missionaries mixed pragmatical piety with an ability to 'schmooze' the local rulers as they fanned out around the country. Bishop Wilfrid of York, in one example, held a three day drunken revelry with many of the nobility of Northumbria and Mercia to celebrate the dedication of Ripon Cathedral in the 660s. Proselytising in those days came with a hangover it would seem.

It was a crucial time for the establishment of the Church and it was around this time that Christianity arrived in Staffordshire. It is difficult however to disentangle the myth and reality in the lives of the local Saints. I was pondering on this whilst visiting the shrine to St Bertram or Bertellinus at Ilam Church.

Bertram, so the story goes, was of royal blood and, having fallen out with his father, fled to Ireland where he fell in love with a princess. She became pregnant and they escaped to England sheltering in the dense forests that surrounded Ilam in the 7th century. Alexander, a monk writing in the 13th century, takes up the story:

'They were in hiding in a dense forest when lo ! the time of her childbirth came upon them suddenly ; born of pain and river of sorrow ! A pitiful child bed indeed ! While Bertellinus went out to get the necessary help of a midwife the woman and her child breathed their last amid the fangs of wolves. Bertellinus on his return imagined that this calamity had befallen because of his own sin, and spent three days in mourning rites'.

That was the turning point in his life; he retired from the world and became a hermit. Bertram is linked with Stafford where he preached, converting the heathen. Then he returned to live in one of the caves beside the river Dove. After his death his remains were buried at Ilam.

The shrine itself is in the Lady Chapel. It is in the form of an altar tomb made about 1386, when a blind Ilam man, named Wilmot, prayed to Bertram and recovered his sight. People still leave requests for prayers on the shrine. I saw prayers of intercession.

Amongst them people who had lost their faith, a sick relative and one for a woman from Birmingham who had taken her own life, placed on the shrine.

IN THE AFTERMATH OF CIVIL WAR

This is an episode from the bloody aftermath of the American Civil War, which caught in its snares a Leek woman who had moved to the United States with the intention of starting a new life in a community with people of like mind.

The story was carried in a Leek paper of May 1885 with the eye-catching headlines:

'A Terrible Adventure'

'A Leek Woman and her Husband shot'

'The Shooters Lynched'

The Leek woman who was subject to this assassination attempt was Mrs Dickenson, whose maiden name was Bromley. She had at one point lived in Church Street before marrying and moving to the States, arriving in New York in 1882. The Dickensons were one of 12 English families who set out West with the idea of forming a socialist commune in Texas. Throughout the 19ᵗʰ century there were many attempts to found communities, such as New Harmony in Connecticut by Robert Owen or the fictitious community that appears in *Martin Chuzzlewit* by Dickens, and of course there exist today religious communities such as the Amish who live in the states of Ohio and Pennsylvania.

The party of settlers arrived in Springfield Missouri where four of the group, among them the Dickensons, were tempted by the offer of land in South West Missouri, close to the border with Arkansas in the area of the Ozark Mountains. They arrived in 1883 and settled in the Tanney County area to grow tobacco and coffee, living in a community according to their deeply-held principles of cooperation. Unfortunately they arrived into an area devastated by the Civil War, which despite ending 20 years before was still blighting the area.

In truth, that part of the United States had been in a lawless state for many years prior to the war of 1861-5. The states of Kansas and Missouri were notorious for maundering banditti, some favourable to the continuation of slavery and others not. In the 1870s and 80s their numbers were swollen by discharged soldiers of both North and South with scores to settle and harbouring grievances. The most famous were the James-Younger gang, of fervent confederate sympathies, who fought a ferocious guerrilla war with the authorities and northern sympathisers, whilst robbing banks. However, the gang had broken up after the disastrous Northfield Raid and Jesse James had been shot dead by Bob Ford in St Joseph, Missouri in April 1883.

The downfall of that gang did not put an end to the

lawlessness, and this was especially true of Southern Missouri. In Tanney County, between 1865 and 1885, despite there being 40 murders, no one was bought to justice: it is believed that many of the juries were packed with relatives or Confederate sympathisers. Some residents of the state resolved to tackle the anarchy, one of them, Mr Dickenson, by use of violence if required. A group led by the imposing Nat Kinney, who was six foot six inches tall, formed a vigilante posse, who were called the 'Bald Knobbers'. They met secretly on the mountaintops of the Ozark Mountains posting sentries on the rocky outcrops of the peaks, from whence they acquired their nickname.

It was a violent crime against the Dickenson's that led to the first bloodshed. The Dickensons ran a store and post office that Mr Dickenson, who was a great fan of the writer, would later name Dickens. The store was based at the isolated community of Eglington. The Dickensons got into a dispute with a pair of vicious young hoodlums called Frank and Tubal Taylor, who were supported in their crime wave by Elijah Sublet. The row was over credit for a pair of boots. The young men reached for their guns as explained in a letter published in the *Leek Times* of the 25th May 1885. Mr Dickenson described what happened.

'Just after 7 pm, Frank Taylor entered the Post Office. I was sitting on a bench by the fireplace outside the counter.... He took hold of me by the throat and said that he had come to settle with me. I got up intending to reach for my pistol, which was just behind the counter. I just got one step and said, "Loose me" when he put his pistol straight in front of my face and fired. Elijah

Sublet and Tubal Taylor were then in the room, and Frank and Tubal tried to drag me out. My wife came to my assistance as soon as she heard the first shot, and as soon as she appeared Frank pointed a pistol at her head and fired. After a little struggle I got released. During the whole of the struggle I heard 4 or 5 shots. The whole affair last a few minutes.

'The first shot entered my upper lip, taking a portion of left jaw and three or four upper teeth; one shot went through Mrs Dickenson's head straightaway, about two inches behind the right ear; another ball went into my right shoulder, steering its way into the right side of my neck; another went through Mrs D's thumb; another went through my coat sleeve, another grazed Mrs D's cheek and eyebrow. Our wounds are not serious'.

The account ended with the information that the young men were intent on murdering the couple as they had fired at their heads. A Hue and Cry was raised for the Taylors. They quickly made their escape and hid in local caves before surrendering to the sheriff on the promise of protection.

The Taylors were locked up in jail in the main town of the area Forsyth. However, what was in store for these unfortunate young men was an invitation to what in the Old West was called a 'Neck Tie Party'. The *New York Times* then takes up the story in an article, which is dated 10th December 1885

At about 10pm the following night a band of men, estimated about 150, rode into the town and posted their guards at different points and with sledge hammers, forced open the jail doors. The two Taylors begged piteously for their lives, but all to no purpose. They were quickly marched out and taken away. The next morning their bodies were found hanging to the limb of a scrub oak tree two and a half miles west of town. It was generally believed that the Bald Knobbers did the lynching.

After that incident the violence and the numbers of vigilantes grew, although others dropped out of the Bald Knobbers, sickened by the lynching of the Taylors. The gangs became more harsh and sought to impose their own will on the community seeking to correct such 'lawlessness', as gamblers, couples who lived in sin or 'loose' women, into changing their ways. Sometimes they intimidated those who spoke out against the vigilantes or who were considered 'ornery'. About 18 people were killed for speaking against the gang. The gang swaggered around the local counties and began to act as despots themselves. They began to alienate former supporters. Many people in Southern Missouri began to see them as tyrants and felt the call to resist.

A reaction set in and groups of armed men called 'anti Bald Knobbers' were formed to oppose the vigilantes. In 1887 the Bald Knobbers attacked families of men who were critical of them. Shotgun blasts and explosions were directed at family cabins. The cries of the women and children brought neighbours to the scene of carnage as two men were shot to death and others, including children, injured. This caused a national outrage and action to catch the vigilante bands that were roaming the state. Eventually, 20 members of the gang were arrested. Four were sentenced to death and clumsily executed.

A member of the anti Bald Knobbers murdered the leader of the Bald Knobbers, Kinney, in August 1888 and was found not guilty at a subsequent trial on the grounds of self-defence. The bloodshed and the intimidation petered out by the end of the century, although the events left much bitterness in local communities.

The story did, however, achieve a national prominence with the publication in 1907 of a novel depicting the events. Harold Bell Wright's *The Shepherd of the Hills* became a best seller. In fact, it was the first American novel to sell one million copies. A silent film was also made of the book in 1919. Southern Missouri became a tourist attraction on the strength of the history, attracting five million Americans a year to theme parks that play out the events in a family-friendly way.

As for the Dickensons, they opened a bigger store by the end of the 1880s, about a mile from their close brush with death. The Post Office Dickens remained open till 1952. Mr Dickenson became a successful businessman, later a judge and a prominent local member of the Republican Party in Missouri.

AUDEN AND FROGHALL

" **H**e would have liked the area. It would have had the sort of landscape that he enjoyed." a biographer of the poet Wystan Hugh Auden told me when I asked about a visit he made to the area as a young man of 18 in 1925. This year sees the 100th anniversary of his birth and certainly the anniversary has lead to an assessment of the man and his work.

Auden is now considered to be one of the greatest poets of the 20th century and twice since his death in 1973 he has resonated posthumously in the public mind. Firstly, when in the 90s film *Four Weddings and a Funeral* John Hannah reads *Funeral Blues* 'Stop all the clocks' over the coffin of Simon Callow. And again, in 2001, he became the unofficial Poet Laureate of New York after the 9/11 attacks in his poem *September 1st 1939* when the lines 'the unmentionable odour of death, offends the September night' and the ending 'we must love each other or die' became a focus for communal grief.

I have always been interested in his work. I found

his work intellectual as well as accessible. An anthology of Auden was the first poetry book that I bought as a teenager. I was particularly impressed by the poem *Shield of Achilles* which details the powerlessness of an onlooker in a totalitarian regime I still have a copy of the book. It has a picture of him as an old man staring out with the heavily wrinkled face that he described as looking like a 'wedding cake left out in the rain'.

Although he was born in Yorkshire, Auden had many links with the Midlands. He moved to Birmingham at the age of 2 when his father became the Director of Public Health in Schools. Auden's unusual first name derives from a 9th century Shropshire born Prince who was later canonised. St Wystan's empty tomb is in the Anglo Saxon crypt of Repton church in Derbyshire. His father went to the school in the town and his grandmother lived in the village of Horninglow on the Staffordshire/ Derbyshire border. Auden visited her regularly up to the time of her death in December 1925. He visited earlier in the year, which lead him to explore the rail system of the Moorlands.

At the age of 15 he decided to be a poet, although his family were keen that he become an engineer, and for the next six years he wrote 200 poems. His style was often in imitation of poets that he admired such as TS Eliot, Thomas Hardy and the First World War poet Edward Thomas. The influence of Thomas is particularly marked in the poems that he wrote while visiting the area in the summer of 1925. The early poems *The Canal, Froghall* and *Flowers and the Stationmaster* were written while visiting the area. A later poem mentions Waterhouses.

He was drawn to a certain type of landscape,

especially mines and quarries. His vision of paradise was 'In my Eden we have a few beam engines, saddle tank locomotives, overshot waterwheels and other pieces of obsolete machinery to play with'. He was associated with the area around Alston in Cumbria; the abandoned lead mines in the area full of the archaic machinery that he craved. In fact, the clue that Auden wrote poems about this area came from a book *WH Auden, Pennine Poet* by Alan Myers and Robert Forsythe, published by North Pennine Heritage Trust.

The Froghall Wharf that he visited that summer would still have been busy, but the truth was that it was entering into a period of decline. The limestone quarries had been in operation since the 18th century and a canal to take advantage the industry was opened in 1777. The connection between the quarry and the canal was by a primitive rail system, the first built in the 18th century. The limestone quarried was found to be particularly good in the smelting of iron ore and increasingly large amounts were transported to the ironworks of the Black Country. The 15,000 tons of rock that was being shifted in the late 19th century had increased to 200,000 during the First World War. The stone was also used in agriculture and for the developing chemical industry especially after 1890. In 1885 there were over 100 men listed as working at the wharf. A photograph from 1905 portrays a very harsh environment with steam billowing and obscuring the landscape. It is a bustling scene, with men active and filling the view. Limestone is burnt and loaded on to the barges owned by Brunner Mold & Co.

A newspaper account from 1936 reported that 'Some 50 years ago the basin was a scene of bustling activity with limestone being broken into ballast grades by large groups of men: limestone was burned into agricultural lime. On the other side of the canal brick making was practised and further into the valley coal was mined from galleries running into the valley sides'.

The company that quarried the stone, Thorley and Bowers, was owned and managed by the curiously named Primrose Thorley. He is in a photograph of 1912, tall and moustached, with his boots caked with lime. His dog, Sappho, used to run alongside the carriage between Cheadle and Froghall. However, the peak of production at Froghall Wharf was brief.

After the War the area went into decline. Following a landslip in the early 20s which made access difficult to the quarries, a decision by the Cheshire-based ICI, which was created out of Brunner Mond to develop their own quarries, effectively doomed the industry.

The poem *The Canal, Froghall* begins 'There are no roads except the towpath through the valley' and everyone who knows the area will recognise the remoteness. The canal follows through attractively quiet countryside 'winding in and out among the hill ribs and hollows', There is a rich wildlife in this secluded spot but the peace is disturbed. A barge is pulled by an old horse and walking beside the animal walks an old man humming to himself and puffing on a clay pipe:

'All unaware of what is scattered by their coming.
They go their way and ripples are the only traces
Until the calm returns which everything effaces
And images of trees resume their standing places'

In October 1925, Auden started his degree, originally in Biology, before changing to English. An interest in landscape and industrial heritage stayed with him throughout his life. In the 1930s, he famously collaborated with the composer Benjamin Britten in the 1935 documentary film *Night Mail* and continued this fascination right to the publication of *Lullaby* the year before his death. Unlike many writers, his reputation has not diminished since his death in 1973.

BETJEMAN AND A LOVE FOR LEEK

John Betjeman liked this area and for a period of around ten years made frequent trips to North Staffordshire. He came to Leek often. The minute book of the Arts Club mentions three visits in 1953, 1958 and finally in April 1960. That visit made the front page of the *Leek Post and Times*. He was pictured with the officers of the club wearing a trademark hat and beaming at the camera.

The visit on 4th April 1960 is not recorded, perhaps it was a courtesy visit. There is no report of a meeting or an address to the club. He liked the town and, in September 1956 in a letter to the recently-appointed Principal of Keele University, George Barnes, he wrote that 'Leek is quite the best town anywhere and the Norman Shaw Church with Lethaby fittings and Hamilton Jackson paintings is finer than its counterpart at Ilkley'.

He liked the people of the area as well. Several months earlier when he congratulated Barnes on obtaining his post at Keele, he commended the area by saying "I love Stoke on Trent and people of the Trent valley are the nicest in England and the toofer, the naicer".

There were a number of reasons why he was drawn to this area during this decade. He had a friend who lived in Leek, DB (Charles) Peace, who was the chief planning officer for Staffordshire County Council and who introduced him to many of the buildings and landscape of the Moorlands. He was very friendly with Peace's wife and tried to help her literary career. In March 1956 he wrote to Longman's publisher pressing the case for the publication of a journal that she had written about Leek during the 1950s, describing it as a 'wonderful record of what life in a provincial town is like. A sort of modern Flora Thompson'. Longman's declined to publish Mrs JM Peace's work on Leek. I wonder what happened to it? Do any readers know? Betjeman reveals his High Anglican distaste and possible snobbery for nonconformity in the letter, 'this was the first work by an articulate Congregationalist that I had heard'.

Mrs Peace's husband was an enthusiast for Staffordshire Churches and wrote the introduction to the county in *Collins Guide to the English Parish Church* published in 1958 with illustrations by John Piper. I have a battered, well-thumbed copy bought in a second hand bookshop in Stratford on Avon in the 1990s. The concluding remarks by Peace in the introduction are apposite and to the point:

'In landscape and architecture Staffordshire is a good average with numerous high spots. There is quite remote country especially in the centre and the north; there is much industrialised building in parts and both in the towns and the countryside there are many churches which deserved to be loved more widely'.

They are places listed in Betjeman's book, sometimes with gnomic descriptions. Alstonefield 'pleasant setting with box pews', Checkley 'the best medieval church in North Staffordshire', Cheddleton with its Burne Jones glass and Rushton 'a church of rare interest and individuality' and Grindon a three word entry 'spire, massings, setting'. The longest entry however is for All Saints in Leek 'a nice contrast between the intimate scale and great arches' and a special mention for the 'splendid green marble font'.

Another reason for visiting the area was Betjeman's long-term friendship with George Barnes, which dated back to 1930 when Barnes was Head of the Talks Department at the BBC. Barnes later become head of the Third Programme and used Betjeman frequently in programmes on heritage and architecture. He discerned in Betjeman a great ability to communicate with a showman's ability to describe to the public some of the architecture and landscapes on offer in Britain. Barnes played a pivotal role in introducing Betjeman to the British public, initially through the radio and as the 50s progressed, on the new medium of TV.

In 1956, Barnes was appointed to a senior academic role at Keele and the poet was a frequent visitor, praising the local towns both in the Potteries and beyond. Betjeman passed on the love of church crawling to Barnes's son Anthony, who in later life became the Director of the Redundant Churches Trust. Later Betjeman was regularly visiting an ailing Barnes and in the words of Betjeman's biographer, AN Wilson, whose book was published in 2006 to commemorate the 100th anniversary of his birth, thought the letters written to Barnes the most impressive things that he wrote.

To Barnes, by this time dying of cancer, he wrote in August 1960:

'Like you, I've spent my life avoiding pain, mental and particularly physical. I know enough however to know how awful pain is, I sometimes think that it is the only thing to reconcile me to dying - to get out of pain... I cannot see that pain serves any purpose except to give one joy and thankfulness for not having it'.

It was a very appealing side of his character that he was very supportive of friends, as well as the anonymous hospital visiting that he carried out meeting and offering support to strangers on regular unpublicised visits to St Bart's in London.

North Staffordshire was very close to Chatsworth House and therein is another reason. Betjeman met Lady Elizabeth Cavendish in memorable circumstances. They met at a dinner party held on 29th May 1951. The event was auspicious for students of espionage as another of the guests of that night, Guy Burgess, had fled a few days earlier to Moscow and another guest that evening, Anthony Blunt, was expected to be arrested at the party. Elizabeth Cavendish was the daughter of the 10th Duke of Devonshire. She was a sister in law of Kitty Kennedy and friend of her brother JFK. At the party Betjeman fell in love with Elizabeth Cavendish and the feeling was reciprocated. It was a relationship that lasted up to his death in 1984. He had been married for many years to Penelope, but it was an unhappy relationship. He spent a great deal of time at Elizabeth's cottage on the Chatsworth estate passing his time 'in rest and quietness' in contrast with the rows at his married home in Berkshire. Early in the relationship he wrote *In Willesden Churchyard, a poem* which describes an illicit affair that the Victorian writer Charles Reade had, using it as an attempt to dissuade the curious. AN Wilson records the morbid fixation that people have about the private lives of others via an illustration:

'Did Laura gently stroke her lover's head?
And did her Charles look into her eyes
For loyal counsel there? I do not know
Doubtless some pedant for his PhD
Has ascertained the facts'.

He was also a regular visitor to Chatsworth from this time onwards so much so that there was a bust of Betjeman placed at the stately home.

Above all, Betjeman liked to gad around Britain. He spent a great deal of time during the 50s and early 60s on the move and involved in campaigns to save the towns and cities of the country from the excesses of architects and planners. In 1957, he founded the Victorian Society, celebrating a period of building and design which at the time was deeply unfashionable.

In 1960, he supported the doomed campaign to save the Euston Arch. I am sure that older readers will recall the arch outside the station. I first went to London in 1961 but, alas, was too young to be aware of this splendid piece of Victoriana. Locally and later on, his support was enlisted in the successful campaign to preserve Cheddleton Railway station, reputedly designed by Pugin, the celebrated Victorian architect. There is probably another reason why Betjeman came to Leek frequently and which explains why there are few records after the early 60s. Betjeman was an enthusiast for the railways, for steam and for branch lines. And of course, Leek's Railway station closed in that decade.

At the end of AN Wilson's book, the Duchess of Devonshire uses the phrase 'blinding charm' about him. I can see that charm deployed to staff and people that he met in Leek as he got off the railway station with his slouched shoulders, his old coat, his battered hat and a beaming smile.

THE MAN IN THE PURPLE GOWN IPSTONES, 1650

Before Rowan Williams, the last bearded Archbishop of Canterbury was the Staffordshire Moorlands born Gilbert Sheldon, who was Archbishop from 1663 to 1677.

Sheldon recounted a curious story to the writer John Aubrey about a strange visitor to the village of Ipstones in the 1650s. A poor, crippled man of the village was disturbed one Sunday by a knock at the door. The stranger asked for a glass of beer, which was given him. The stranger then asked the old man how long he had been ill and told him that he could cure him with a herbal preparation. The old man was told that he must also be pious and fervently serve God. The cure seemed to work, although no one else saw the stranger, who was curiously dressed in a purple shag gown, wandering the lanes of Ipstones. Sheldon intimated that the visitor was the Wandering Jew.

The story of the Wandering Jew, commonly called Ahasuerus or sometimes Cartaphilus, is an ancient one. The legend began to spread in Europe in the 13th century. The original account concerns a Jew who taunted Jesus on the way to the Crucifixion and then was then cursed to walk the earth until Christ returns.

After his fate was declared, he became a penitent Christian who did good deeds and issued pious warnings to the people he encountered.

There were claims of sightings throughout Europe, since at least 1542 in Germany, and up to 1868 in New York. Joseph Jacobs, writing in 1911 commented 'It is difficult to tell in any one of these cases how far the story is an entire fiction and how far some ingenious impostor took advantage of the existence of the myth'.

As a representation the character became symbolic of the fate of a benighted people oppressed over the ages. The figure of the doomed sinner, forced to wander without the hope of rest in death till the millennium, impressed itself upon the popular imagination, and passed thence into literary forms. The Wandering Jew features in work from Chaucer's *Pardoners Tale* onwards. Works by Hans Christian Andersen, the German poet Schiller, Shelley and Alexander Dumas all feature him.

An early photograph of Leek Market Place in the 19th century. Bostock and Wombwell Menagerie would use the square for their shows.

The Nicholson Institute, completed in 1884 and visited by such luminaries as Major Olcott, Baden-Powell and Oscar Wilde.

*Mark Twain who visited Leek in November 1899
during a black period of the Boer War. A resolute
opponent of imperialist wars, whether they be
American or British.*

A
'SHOWILY DRESSED'
WOMAN

I went to see a medium once. I went with a friend of my partner's in a sceptical humour. I had been to a psychic fair once before, where a speaker believed that my natural suspicion was down to the fact I had been a Rabbi in a previous life. I presumed that the audience would be mainly female and elderly.

I was wrong on the second count, as the audience of around 120 was primarily young women. There were five men. I wondered at the time, why are women more likely to be interested in this sort of thing? It seems always to have been the case.

I found an amusing case from a 1908 edition of the *Leek Times*. It concerned a fraudster who set herself up as a fortune-teller, operating from 6 Cromwell Terrace. 'Madame Melbourne' announced her business by means of a card she put in the house window. It read 'Madame Melbourne - Australian and scientific palmist'. Her real name was the prosaic May Tunnicliffe when she appeared before local magistrates on a charge of using palmistry to deceive.

The paper reported that she was 'showily dressed and wearing a quantity of jewellery'.

The three principal witnesses were the wives of local policemen: Mrs Ewell of Wetton and Mrs Salter and Mrs Frost, both of Waterhouses, had all availed themselves of her services. Madame Melbourne was firm in her conclusions and usually wrong. She told a bemused Mrs Salter that she had five children. She was mistaken, but gamely Madame struggled on "You have four children," - again wrong. She seemed to have little luck with Mrs Frost either. Madame Melbourne went on "In three years time you will marry an old man (great laughter) who would love the very ground you walk on and give you everything that you want".

Madame Melbourne informed the court that she had read the hand of the Chairman of Stafford Bench, but local magistrates were less good-natured. The palmist did have supporters in Marie Hall and Mary Harlow, two silk hands who believed the fortune-teller. The bench were unmoved and they fined her.

I wonder if May Tunnicliffe saw that coming?

HUCKLEBERRY FINN COMES TO LEEK

Mark Twain, perhaps America's most distinguished man of letters, visited Leek on Wednesday 29th November 1899. His signature appears in the visitors book of the Nicholson Institute in a very strong hand. Samuel Langhorne Clemens, the real name of Mark Twain, was born on the 30th November 1835. It is therefore possible that he celebrated his 64th birthday in the area. This is a matter for conjecture, because an extensive search of the *Leek Times* has revealed no additional information about the visit and one has to conclude that the trip was a private one.

Mark Twain was one of the most celebrated writers in the world in the 1890s. He had created Tom Sawyer and Huckleberry Finn - two of the best loved and enduring characters in world literature, so the lack of comment in the local press is mystifying. News of this most celebrated of authors would have certainly made the headlines and press coverage ought to have been extensive.

It should be said that Leek at the end of the 19th century was well used to receiving high profile visitors. Indeed, a reading of the newspapers reveals a very rich cultural and political heritage. In October 1899, the pioneer of investigative journalism who would later die on the Titanic, WT Stead, spoke at a well-attended anti-Boer war rally in the town and in December the first Labour MP, Keir Hardie, spoke in Leek and was fully reported in the Times.

Twain, when he visited Leek that late autumn day, had endured many tribulations. Since 1895, he had more or less been on a permanent lecturing tour in order to clear debts following the collapse of his publishing firm. The following year his beloved daughter, Susy, died of meningitis at the family home in Connecticut, while Twain was forced through circumstances to stay in England.

Just prior to his visit to Staffordshire, Twain had undergone a health cure in a sanatorium in Sweden where he had stayed for several months before returning to Britain in October 1899. Political essays were his main preoccupation as a writer and what exercised him most were the colonial wars in which both were engaged — America in the Philippines and Britain in a war in South Africa - the Boer War. Twain was bitterly opposed to both military adventures. He had a card printed, which bore the slogan:

'I bring you the stately maiden called CHRISTENDOM - returning bedraggled, besmirched and dishonoured from pirate raids in South Africa and the Philippines; with her soul full of meanness, her pockets full of boodle and her mouth full of pious hypocrisies. Give her soap and towel, but hide the looking glass'.

The *Leek Times* in late November was full of news from the South African War and one can make an assumption that as a journalist himself Twain might have read the edition. The newspaper printed the previous Saturday, 25th November was full of bad news. The British were suffering reversals in places, which would become very well known - Kimberley, Belmont, and Colenso. A small news item in the paper noted the capture of a journalist named Winston Churchill, following an attack on an armoured train. A Leek man was wounded at the Battle of Modder River.

The Boer War certainly divided opinion in Leek. The architect, Larner Sugden, wrote a lengthy letter defending the Boers describing them as 'intrepid peasants' for which he received much obloquy. The war was going so badly that the reservists were being called up. In fact a childhood memory my grandmother had, as a nine year old, was of soldiers in their red coats marching to Stoke Station on their way to war.

Further delving into the newspapers of the time uncovers fascinating snippets of information. Interestingly, there is a review of a novel called *One Hour and the Next* by Millicent, Duchess of Sutherland, on the conditions of the mills in Leek, largely written in dialect. The Duchess herself would be fictionalised in Arnold Bennet's *The Card*. And, on the subject of fiction and in a story that might have come from the pen of Thomas Hardy, there is a description of an elderly man, in a letter recounting a boyhood incident when he visited a witch who lived in Russell Street. She would discourage the many black witches in the town by throwing a 'dashun' of salt into the fire when one passed.

A perusal of the pages would rapidly disabuse you of the notion that this was a golden age for children. Mortality was very high, whether it is through disease or by accident. Clarice Burgess, aged eight, of Garden Street was killed when she was hit in the head by a wooden seat of a swing while playing on Westwood Recreational Grounds. Arthur Sheldon, nine, was sentenced to three strokes of the birch for annoying Mr JPF Smith of King Street, by ringing his doorbell frequently.

The sports writer for the *Times* seemed to have a Twain-like sardonic turn of phrase describing a poor season for Leek Town: 'the unexpected happened on Saturday last Leek actually won a game and against the Congleton Hornets'.

Many of the stories had almost a modern ring and the late Victorian's were equally concerned with lawlessness and excessive drinking. Writing in November 1899, the Chief Public Health Officer was deeply concerned at the easy availability of alcohol:

'The returns of the Commissioners of Inland Revenue show on the whole that users of alcohol consume about 25% more than alcohol users of 50 years ago.... English people today do breath less poisons than their fathers and grandfathers did, they voluntary swallow much more'.

Such opinions were supported by a very well organised temperance movement in Leek who were strongly of the view that drink did the poor no good at all. The members of the Leek Board of Guardians put this view into practical action and stopped the one-pint ration of beer for the Christmas dinner of the workhouse inmates.

As Twain himself wrote a few years earlier in *Pudden'head Wilson's Calendar,* 'Nothing so needs reforming as other people's habits.'

EDWARD LEAR AND THE MAN FROM FLASH

Apart from the widely-known example of Charles Dickens, 2012 also marked the 200th anniversary of another literary giant.

Also born in 1812 was Edward Lear, the developer of the limerick. In addition, he was an outstandingly good artist and travel writer with a particular love of the Mediterranean. The limerick is, of course, a witty poem, especially one in five-line meter with a strict rhythm. It is quite an exercise to produce work to this scrupulous meter.

Although he did not invent the form, Lear certainly did a great deal to popularise limericks. Lear had a troubled life. From childhood he endured ill health, including epilepsy, of which he was ashamed, and was affected by depressive illness. He never managed to marry, but he had good friends and doted on his cat, Foss. He was a wandering artist, travelling, despite his paranoia, to wild parts of Europe to make exquisite watercolours. Some of these journeys were risky. Corsica, for instance, was infested with brigands who made a habit of kidnapping solitary travellers. He wrote accounts of these journeys, sketching wherever he went, grumbling about miserable accommodation, boring encounters with German travellers, and also about the monks he found everywhere and detested.

Lear did have North Staffordshire connections. He did the rounds of the aristocratic homes of the area, such as Trentham, where he was appalled by the smoky atmosphere from nearby Stoke.

Simon Daniel, a fellow scribbler in Leek and I believed we should not allow this anniversary to pass unnoticed in the Moorlands, so we produced a few local examples.

> A farmer who lived outside Leek
> Had a prize Dexter bull that could speak
> He taught it good diction
> And fed it pulp fiction
> The classics, pig Latin and Greek

> A vicious young thug from Brown Edge
> Tipped young birds out before they could fledge
> But one day they fought back
> With a vicious attack
> And pecked him to death on a ledge

> A Teutonic zealot from Flash
> In the First War sprouted a 'tash
> He looked like the Kaiser
> He should have been wiser
> And he wouldn't have been run out of Flash.

We did write a limerick regarding a wayward young woman from Tean, but judged it too lewd for the readership of the *Post and Times*.

EVOLUTION v CREATION AT THE SALVATION ARMY

The main claim to fame of the 19th century biologist Alfred Russel Wallace was the part he played in the writing of perhaps the most influential book ever published.

Wallace, a friend of Leek architect Larner Sugden, was studying the fauna of Malaysia in the 1850s when he came up with the idea of natural selection. His insight was independently arrived at. He wrote to Charles Darwin with an idea that closely matched Darwin's own. Darwin's friends urged him to quickly write up his own conclusions on evolution, which led to him completing his book *Origin of the Species*, which was published to instant success in 1859.

The debate around creation and evolution has raged ever since and even in the last few weeks the controversy has continued, with Texas State Board of Education unanimously rejecting a creationist supplement to textbooks, instead voting to endorse science-based ones.

Perhaps we expect the clash between the creationists and the supporters of evolution to be at its most intense in the US although, from personal experience, belief in a biblical interpretation of the history of the Earth remains strong locally. Early in 2010, I went to a public meeting at the Salvation Army. The meeting was well-attended and lengthy: it went on for three hours. The three principal speakers railed against the secular conspiracy that threatened their belief in creationism imposing, in their opinion, the questionable theory of evolution. I spoke, as I believe that there is no incompatibility between science and religion on evolution. I also pointed out the great contribution that clergymen have made to science. I was the only person in a room of 50 who spoke this way.

In retrospect, I found the view expressed in the room, that Christians believe that they are being persecuted, difficult to square with reality. Certainly, during Tony Blair's premiership, faith groups have more involvement in social care and educational provision.

And persecution seems a rather objectionable conclusion to arrive at when compared with the suffering of believers in Nazi Germany and the Soviet Union.

QUEEN OF WITCHES

Cheddleton born Sybil Leek, the self proclaimed 'Queen of the Witches' was a contentious figure and a colourful one as well: her trademarks were a loose-fitting cloak, hoods, a pet jackdaw called Mr Hotfoot Jackson and a snake named Sashima.

Even Sybil's birth date was the subject of some argument. She gave the date as 22nd February 1922, while others set the date at five years earlier. She also claimed to be the reincarnation of the Burslem witch Molly Leigh. Sybil maintained many things in her life, for example that she had a friendship as a child with HG Wells and Lawrence of Arabia.

She was interested in paganism from an early age and was on good terms with Aleister Crowley - the self-proclaimed most evil man in the World. There is a story that Crowley and Leek visited Burslem to seek out Molly Leigh's grave - a jackdaw perched on Leek's shoulders. After the war, Leek went to the United States and became a media star, appearing on TV shows. She met and married a man named Brian.

Sybil was also involved with a number of American celebrities including Ronald Reagan, who maintained an interest in clairvoyance throughout his life. She also had a friendship with the writer Robert Bloch, best known for his novel *Psycho*.

She believed that she could predict events and scored an undoubted hit with a prediction she made in the early 70s.

'There is one menace to the career and potential of George Wallace' - the candidate for the American presidency in 1972, Leek asserted in her *Astrological Guide to the Presidential Candidates*.

'The nearer he gets to his goal, the greater the danger of political assassination'.

Written in early 1971, these words were of more interest to horoscope buffs than to political ones. But when Arthur Bremer, nearly 18 months later, fulfilled the prophecy and shot Wallace, crippling the Governor of Alabama, some political pundits decided to take a closer look at what was written in the candidates' stars.

Not that Leek's peeks into the future always proved entirely accurate. She once predicted, for example, that in 1970 President Richard Nixon would become embroiled in a sex scandal that would jeopardise his re-nomination by Republicans. But she failed entirely to predict Watergate, which really did bring Nixon down.

ROGER MORRICE AND HIS 'ENTIRING BOOK', 1688

The diary of Alistair Campbell has been the subject of much comment in the media following its publication. The newspapers, both broadsheet and tabloid, expended a great deal of ink in covering the thoughts of the spin master at the heart of New Labour and the man who had the ear of the most senior politicians of our time. He has been interviewed by both the new and old media.

Campbell's diary, from the reviews I have read, would appear to be self-serving and uncritically endorsing the actions of the powerful while despising the powerless. This perhaps adds another mark to the general lack of esteem in which politicians are held. Certainly they portray the leaders of today to be vacuous, foul-mouthed and lacking in insight

However, the use of the diary as a vehicle for self-justification and name checking is a new phenomenon. In the golden age of the diarist in the 17th century, the purpose of the diary was completely different.

The diary of Samuel Pepys, perhaps the most famous English diarist, was written in code which was only cracked centuries after his death. It is the diary of a near contemporary of Pepys, a person called Roger Morrice who was born in the Staffordshire Moorlands, which was also partly written in code which has excited interest in academic circles.

Roger Morrice was born in 1628 in Meerbrook and returned to die in the village in 1702. Morrice was a puritan minister who was the minister at one time at a parish in Duffield in Derbyshire before moving to London. Like Campbell, he became a political journalist who was extremely well placed and privy to some of the main political stories of his time. Morrice wrote down many of his entries in a form of shorthand into a number of 'entiring' books which were bought by a religious library in the 18th century and for centuries simply gathered dust. The Entiring Books comprise of a million words and cover the period 1677 to 1691; one of the most turbulent periods of English History. He would have reached his early adulthood during the Civil War where religious intolerance was common and hatred, especially of Catholics, was frequently expressed. It was a time that the most feared country was Catholic France, which in the later 17th century was at the peak of its power.

Morrice was an extreme Protestant and, unlike the more relaxed and hedonistic Pepys, took a firm moral view of his times. He described Tunbridge Wells, then a very fashionable town popular with royalty and the aristocracy, as the most debauched town in the country. With a great deal of approval he reported the reaction of the Moroccan ambassador at the court of Charles II, when he was urged to 'receive a whore into his bed'.

'He said to our great rebuke and shame "My religion forbids whores, does not yours?" When I come home I shall be counted a liar in my own country, for my master will not believe me that so many ladies came open faced with bare breasts to see me?'

During the late 17th century, the River Thames often froze and fairs were held on the ice. In 1684, the frozen surface was able to bear coaches, which travelled on the ice. Other activities including bull baiting and bonfires were held on the river. Morrice did not approve: 'The concourse and all manner of debauchery upon the Thames continued on the Thames upon the Lord's Day and Monday the 4th and 5th of this instant'.

The 1680s saw three different monarchs on the throne and it was a time of the greatest suspicion and plotting as rival groups sought to establish power over other factions at court. Morrice wrote in code because he wished to protect his source at the centre of power, believed by modern day researchers to have been a member of the cabinet. A team from Cambridge University transcribed the diaries and produced a number of volumes, which were published in 2005.

The diary describes in great depth the events that brought about the overthrow of James II and the successful revolt that led to William III assuming power in 1688. Morrice was ferociously anti-Catholic and was appalled by the birth of a son to Catholic James in June 1688.

'The child was a large full child in the head and the upper parts but not suitably proportioned in the lower parts,' wrote Morrice.

Six months later James was deposed in perhaps the most successful coup d'état ever seen in British history and, on the last occasion when England was invaded by a foreign power, Dutch troops marched on London in December, as James fled the country. James II's grandson, Charles Edward Stuart, would, over 50 years later, return and play a part in the history of the Moorlands by leading the Highland Army through the area during December 1745.

Morrice wrote that women, 'shook the soldiers by the hand as they came by and cried, 'Welcome, welcome, God bless you came to redeem our religion, laws, liberties and lives''.

He returned to North Staffordshire before his death in 1702 and left £100 to the church in Meerbrook for the purchase of bibles and the education of eight poor children in Latin. He also left £20 to a Josiah Hargreaves to run a Presbyterian Meeting House in Westwood after his death. Hargreaves was still at Westwood in 1716.

Morrice's diary describes the politics of over 300 years ago. It is questionable whether the Campbell diaries will have the same longevity and they are certainly written in a far less elegant style. Morrice's words carry with them a certain resonance that should have served as a warning to the politicians and placemen like Campbell who played such a pivotal role in involving us in the Iraqi war:

'For men of power are so void of sense and reason, their cares are not open with patience to hear men of little passion, greater sense and consideration'.

THE
RUSHTON
MUTILATION, 1879

When two farmers, Johnson and Clowes, left the Fox Inn at Rushton Spencer on a snowy December night in 1879, they thought little of the future ramifications over an argument concerning the sale of geese with another local farmer named Brooks. The pair met Brooks on the road that night and Johnson realised that Brooks was still annoyed at being outbid by him for the birds.

But in Johnson's account, nothing was really said and the men went home. A day or so later Johnson heard that Brooks had been attacked. Although in the demure way of the press of the time, this was not the whole of it, as Brooks had been castrated by an unknown assailant. Johnson thought that when the police called a day or so later that he would be called as a witness having seen Brooks prior to the assault. It turned out that the police had arrived to arrest both men on a charge of grievous assault. The judicial process was speedy and both men found themselves in the dock by the end of January 1880. They were found guilty.

Johnson, in a subsequent interview, was very contemptuous of the lack of guidance and support by his legal team. Johnson and Clowes got ten years penal servitude. They rigorously protested their innocence and began to serve a prison term firstly at Pentonville and then at Chatham. It was hard at first as they were in solitary confinement and the two men were used to the outdoor life. The regime was a severe one and the two men were put to work in menial back-breaking work. Johnson did not feel any bitterness to Brooks for allowing this situation to develop. Johnson gained some solace from the prison chaplain at Pentonville 'But many a night I burst my eyes thinking about it'. The poor diet and toil reduced both men to shadows of their former selves, physically and mentally.

Clowes added a statement 'Our conviction came on us sudden. We could not blame the jury or the judge, for no one at the trial had anything to say for us and Brooks' words were not contradicted'.

The two men's luck changed when Brooks died and in a death bed confession insisted that the two men were innocent. Brooks had in fact wounded himself. The Home Secretary ordered their release and the two men were given a change of clothing and put on a train to North Staffordshire. They were well treated and spent some time in Burslem, where the Mayor of the town gave them money before the men went to their homes.

Mrs Clowes told the press that the family had been broken up and she had been turned out of the farm. The children were living with other relatives and she now ran a shop on Biddulph Moor. Johnson had been much changed by the experience.

SIR PHILIP'S
MISSING TOE

Most people celebrate their 21st birthday with family and friends in some comfortable place, a pub, a restaurant or on holiday. Sir Philip Brocklehurst of Swythamley Park near Leek was somewhat different. He chose to celebrate his 21st on March 5th 1908, in a party that was attempting to climb Mount Erebus, at 12,448 feet, the world's most southerly active volcano. On that day, he was sheltering in a sleeping bag with two others.

Photographs taken show the 4000 foot column of smoke and steam billowing around the volcano. He was one of a party of six pulling a sledge that weighed 600 pounds. How the young man found himself in this situation and what happened to the 1907-9 expedition is an adventure worthy of being described as a ripping yarn.

Brocklehurst's fate, born on 5th March 1887, was linked with one of the country's greatest polar explorers Ernest Shackleton, 13 years older than the baronet. Along with Robert Falcon Scott, the

Norwegians Amundsen and Nansen, and the American Peary, he is one of the greats in the Golden Age of Polar Exploration. When they first met, the Irishman had achieved fame as being part of an expedition which got nearest to the South Pole. Known to the people who worked with him as 'the Boss', Shackleton displayed excellent leadership abilities throughout his life, which were tested in the extreme conditions of polar exploration. He also combined the characteristics of man of action and meditative man, as he was a voracious reader and he loved poetry. At his welcoming dinner in June 1909, Shackleton quoted lines from Keats, wholly in keeping with the occasion, to illustrate the courage and the doggedness that the men under his command had exhibited.

His early life at sea equipped him to be accepted on the Discovery expedition to the South Pole in 1902, led by Robert Falcon Scott. There was a personality clash between the two men and, while the *Discovery* expedition was successful in that they got further south than anyone before, they were still 533 miles short of their objective. After returning to Britain, Shackleton began to raise funds in an attempt to reach the South Pole. He had maintained good connections with the Royal Geographic Society which enabled him to be successful when a competition to reach the South Pole was opened by the Society in early 1907. Shackleton had been making contacts to raise money. However, lack of funding was to remain a constant problem right up to the start of the expedition.

Ernest Shackleton met Brocklehurst in the London flat of an American acquaintance, Miss Haveymeyer, in 1906. Shackleton was rather vague about the details of the expedition to the South Pole. However, the young baronet was enthusiastic and volunteered his services at once. At that time Brocklehurst had just left Cambridge. He was, in the language of the time, regarded as 'hearty', interested in sport. He was a good boxer and, at Cambridge, he acquired a Half Blue. After leaving University, he failed to take his degree; he continued to box, ultimately sparring with Champions Jimmy Wilde and Bombardier Billy Wells. Both Brocklehurst and Shackleton would express their great interest in the sport, and at the end of the voyage the younger man noted the excitement he felt on discovering the outcome of the heavyweight boxing championship fight between Jack Johnson - the black American challenger - and Canadian Tommy Burns. (In later life Brocklehurst was a patron of a boxing club in Macclesfield.)

Shackleton was doubly-impressed by Brocklehurst's wealth and his physical prowess. Sir Philip caused Shackleton some concerns on the grounds that he was 'one for the ladies', 'Bohemian' and 'extravagant with taxis' and he had his doubts. The meeting, it turned out, was a great success and Shackleton and Brocklehurst remained life-long friends. I have the impression that the older man was a father figure to Sir Philip. He was also influenced by Shackleton's leadership style. The expedition leader was a good communicator. He had the ability to treat the men as if they were all individually important. His spirit of optimism and transparent honesty made him a natural and personable 'Boss'.

Brocklehurst offered to help pay for the expedition although he was only 19 and had no control over the family finances. His mother held the purse strings. Shackleton met with Lady Brocklehurst and so charmed her that money was found to assist in funding the expedition. He was keen that the young man assisted the expedition in a practical way as well as offering the undoubted drive and stamina:

'take up a course of practical surveying; learn to take your latitudes and longitudes with a theodolite. Learn to take your bearings with a compass. Learn to take a survey with a planer table. Take up a course in field geology. Learn to recognise the particular formations of rocks... Learn the particular sedimentary, volcanic and igneous rocks.'

More importantly, when the fitting out of the *Nimrod* - a Dundee built whaler - was proving to be a financial burden on Shackleton, he was able to call on Brocklehurst's financial support to guarantee £2,000. Later on, Brocklehurst's contacts with the Scottish author Campbell Mackellar would prove equally beneficial to the outcome of the expedition. His cousin also had useful social connections. John Fielden Shackleton was equerry to Queen Alexandria and was able to gain royal patronage for the voyage. King Edward VII visited the *Nimrod* before they embarked.

Sir Philip joined the expedition late and was unhurried, spending some time in Australia watching an Ashes Test match in Sydney during Christmas 1907. He saw George Gunn of Nottinghamshire make 119 in his first Test Match, although Australia went on to win the match by two wickets. Brocklehurst joined the party in Christchurch.

The voyage took several weeks to reach South Victoria Land. The expedition had to endure mountainous seas shortly after they left New Zealand on New Year's Day 1908. They sighted their first iceberg on 14th January and the following day the ship encountered pack ice. Shackleton feared that they would become trapped and altered course for the McMurdo Sound; they landed at the end of the month at Cape Royds. The weather was atrocious and stores were buried under several feet of snow and ice. The first task that the expedition decided on was the conquest of the unclimbed Mount Erebus in early March 1908.

Brocklehurst was to take part in the ascent despite having little experience of climbing. Blizzards blew and the snow was described by one of the expedition members as being very fine and gritty, whipping into the faces of the mountaineers. The temperature dropped in the final stage of the ascent to minus 34 degrees.

The final party to attempt the summit was made up of three of Brocklehurst's comrades, Edgeworth David, Mawson and Mackay, with Brocklehurst and two others as support. The group was provisioned with ten days of supplies. Below the volcano a fierce blizzard blew up and the men sheltered in three man sleeping bags, much criticised by David as being very uncomfortable and affording little protection or comfort. Brocklehurst complained that often on waking he would find his mouth full of fibres.

'Everything is covered with these little hairs about an inch long out of our Reindeer sleeping bags. The other night I turned the bag inside out and shook it, but it is every bit as bad if not worse'.

Sleep deprivation was something that all the

participants on the expedition complained about especially as men were snoring and moving about trying to get comfortable. At some point Brocklehurst emerged from the sleeping bag to answer a call of nature. It was an action that nearly proved calamitous. The force of the wind was strong enough to blow him half way down a chasm. Another of the party was also swept down the mountain and after a struggle was able to reach the safety of the group. The blizzard lasted for a day. After it had subsided Brocklehurst complained that his feet felt cold. His feet were examined and it was discovered that both big toes had been attacked by frostbite. He was in some discomfort and it was decided to leave him behind while the others successfully climbed the summit. A month later, at base camp, one of his frost-bitten big toes was amputated.

After this initial accomplishment the expedition then split up into three groups to carry out specific tasks. The Northern Party's task was to reach the magnetic South Pole; Shackleton led the Southern Party whose objective was the South Pole, while the Western Party, including Sir Philip, surveyed mountains around McMurdo Sound, discovering the potential for economic exploitation of minerals. Earlier, Shackleton had suggested that Brocklehurst be a part of the larger Southern team, but the conditions of his toes forced a change of mind. The Western Party were carried 16 miles by the car that had been bought out - a first in Polar exploration.

The Arrol-Johnson performed very well. The oil was specifically developed to withstand temperatures down to minus 30F. Ordinary tyres with skid-chains were found to be adequate and operated excellently in the conditions. This was 100 years before Clarkson and May attempted a polar excursion in a Toyota Hilux along with film crew, sat nav and with emergency services to hand. On the way back from dropping off Brocklehurst and the others, the car got stuck in ice crevices and was not used again. In the thawing ice it was thought too dangerous.

Brocklehurst began to have strange dreams, which reveal the sense of insecurity that he and the others must have felt. He dreamed

'that the ponies died early and Shackleton was unsuccessful, while Mackay sat on Butter Point when we arrived back explaining how he had quarrelled with the Professor and Mawson and the rope had broken while the Professor and Mawson were on some very thin ice. About as ill-omened a dream as I ever heard'.

At first the group achieved their tasks and the three men collected minerals and fossils, as well as surveying a previously unknown part of Antarctica. They enjoyed breakfasting on Skua eggs, as the birds were a terrible nuisance, both to the men and dogs. Brocklehurst, despite having an amputated toe, climbed a small mountain - Harbour Heights - and was able to keep a note on the surrounding topography.

On 25th January 1909 their lives were placed in peril when the ice they were camping on broke off and floated along the coast. There was the risk of being carried off into the open sea and the danger of killer whales. Brocklehurst and his comrades were in a dilemma, but the only course open to them was to remain on the floe and await a passing ship or the hope that they might drift back to land. The men had good fortune, as the following day the ice had drifted very close to the shore and they were able to jump off the floe.

The ice floe then drifted back into the open sea. Brocklehurst commented on a disappointed group who had been recent observers:

'The killer whales were all around the foot of the glacier, great ugly brutes deprived of their unusual breakfast'.

He had cheated death for a second time.

The Northern Party, under the command of Edgeworth David, reached the magnetic pole, despite suffering appallingly in blizzards and temperatures below minus 20F, and were, like Brocklehurst's party, picked up by the *Nimrod*. Shackleton, leading the Southern party, passed the previous record for most southerly point set by Scott during the *Discovery* expedition of six years earlier and on 9th January 1909 planted the Union flag 97 miles from the South Pole. Disappointed, the group turned back for their rendezvous with the *Nimrod*.

Nimrod returned to Britain in June 1909 and Shackleton, Brocklehurst and the rest of the crew were feted at a Royal Geographic Society dinner. Shackleton, in responding to the toast, said that the reception that the crew had received in New Zealand and Australia had been a very fulsome one and had prepared them for the welcome they received in London. He congratulated the crew on their devotion to duty. They had had a miraculous escape, but they were ready to return to Antarctica. Brocklehurst enjoyed being feted and made much of his missing toe. At another dinner at the Savage Club chaired by

Scott, he was at the centre of attention. Scott asked what had happened to the toe: "I hear he has bought the toe back in a bottle".

Brocklehurst informed the gathering that it was doing the rounds of London Medical Schools examined by clinicians interested in the effect of frostbite. "I wish I had it. I can't regain possession of my toe. The Doctors want it".

The *Leek Times* of 19th June 1909 devoted an editorial to the safe return of the *Nimrod*. Shackleton felt that to turn back only 100 miles from the Pole was the correct thing to do. "We could do no more," he said. The editorial praised the actions of the party, "they had touched the limit of human endurance". No mention was made of the local connection that Sir Philip had with the area.

Shackleton went to Antarctica in 1914 in the Endurance expedition. The voyage proved to be nearly disastrous. After the ship was crushed by ice, the expedition was forced on an epic journey of survival. Despite suffering much hardship, all the crew were rescued, after an ordeal that lasted ten months. Shackleton died at the age of 47 in January 1922. He was buried on the South Atlantic island of South Georgia.

Sir Philip was to continue a life of public service up to his death on 28th January 1975. He married in 1913; Shackleton was best man. During the First World War, Sir Philip served in the Life Guards. He was wounded. In the early 1920s, he worked with the Egyptian Army and achieved the rank of Lieutenant Colonel. An interesting aspect of his life was his involvement in Military Intelligence in the mid 1930s, keeping an eye on far right groups including his North Staffordshire neighbour and British Union of Fascists' leader, Sir Oswald Mosley at Wootton. In the Second World War he commanded a mechanised brigade of the Arab Legion and was British Consul in Trans-Jordan between 1943-4. He chaired Swythamley Parish Council for over 50 years. He was also very active in the Conservative Party.

He was devoted to his brother, Henry Courtney Brocklehurst, who was killed in action in Burma in 1942. Philip inscribed an epitaph on Hanging Stone Rock to his memory. Henry shared his brother's outside life: he hunted game in East Africa and wrote an account of his time as a warden for the Sudanese Government. His book *Game Animals of the Sudan* written in 1931 is dedicated to Philip. Henry went on to set up the wild life sanctuary on the Roaches before the Second World War, which was continued by his brother after Henry's death. In the late 40s, a Tibetan yak wandered the estate and a friend of mine came head to head with one when climbing in the area. The wallabies were a result of this enterprise.

A story circulated about the fate of Brocklehurst's big toe after he had recovered it from a London teaching hospital. It had a place of honour on the mantelpiece at Swythamley Park and disappeared after his death. The yarn went that a guest ate it thinking it was a snack at the wake for Sir Philip.

In October 2007, the *Times* carried a report that the descendents of members of the Nimrod expedition were to follow in the steps of their forebears and attempt to reach the South Pole, amongst them Patrick Bergil, the great grandson of Ernest Shackleton. The expedition was to begin on 28th October 2008 and was being used to launch a Shackleton Foundation, which will fund projects that embody the spirit of leadership and adventure personified in Ernest Shackleton and the men who followed him 100 years ago.

∽

THE LEGACY OF WILLIAM MORRIS

R eading through the archives of the *Post and Times,* I stumbled across the obituary of someone whose fame continues to grow throughout the world over 100 years after his death and is, perhaps, the most notable figure to live in Leek in the last 130 years.

The *Leek Times* of 10th October 1896 carried the sad news of the death of William Morris who had died a week earlier. His doctor believed his early death at the age of 62 was caused by doing the work of ten men. He had worked himself to death. It was noted in the *Times* article that Morris, the internationally renowned artist, designer, educationist, environmentalist, writer and Socialist propagandist was well known in the town. He last came to Leek in December 1882, when he gave a public lecture in conjunction with the School of Art.

A number of telegrams were sent to Jane Morris, his widow, from a variety of notable citizens in Leek such as the architect Larner Sugden. The previous

Tuesday, the Leek Working Men's Reading and Debating Union passed a resolution recording their grief and loss at the death of such a brave and brilliant champion of Labour.

The obituary notice described the principal role that Morris had in the development of art and design in the later half of the 19th century especially in the influence of the Pre-Raphaelite Movement. The obituary notices in the *Leek Times* was signed Walter Crane, who included a poem that he had written for the occasion. Both Sugden and Crane would ensure that Morris's name would live on in Leek and the impact of one of the great figures of the 19th century would continue to play a role in progressive politics in the town well into the next century.

Morris's interest in Leek was the consequence of an interest in returning to the colours in dyes derived from natural materials. He came to the town a number of times from February 1875 onwards, sometimes staying for several weeks whilst working with Thomas Wardle, the brother-in-law of his works manager George, at his dye works at Hencroft.

Morris was faced with working conditions that were the consequences of industrialisation. He regarded one of the worst aspects of factories as being the tendency to chain workers to a single repetitive task. In a lecture of the 1880s, Morris would describe the modern factory as 'a temple of overcrowding and overwork'. His anti-factory system writings drew on his Leek experience. For the first time he came across the social consequences of capitalism and its impact upon people. The poor huddled together beside gigantic factories in houses the size of dog kennels. He also saw the spoiling of rivers and the increase in atmospheric pollution which, he concluded, were the consequence of unrestricted capitalism.

The 19th century had a profound impact upon Leek; in the 1870s its population had tripled since the beginning of the century. This growth in its textile industry would result in it becoming one of the centres of the British silk industry.

At the start of his first stay, Morris' initial opinion about Leek was favourable. He thought the town not nearly as bad as he anticipated and in a letter to his wife described the countryside around as being beautiful. He lodged with the Wardles in their substantial house in St Edward Street.

Morris became obsessed with the goal of producing perfect, original colours naturally. Both Wardle and Morris spoke to older dyers who remembered how they did things before synthetic dyes were introduced. Morris would write back to friends and family, chronicling the experiments and the search for natural dyes that he and Wardle were enthusiastically embarking upon, but it was the search for the perfect blue that dominated Morris's time and energy.

He became an expert at the process, one could almost say obsessive, knowledgeable on the problems of oxidation and identifying the smell of 'stinking meat' which indicated that the dye was ready. He was 'hands on' in this hunt and when he returned to London it amused his friends to discover that his hands were bright blue. It caused embarrassment to him when he was out and about in the capital and he was nervous about gaining admission to the premier of Gilbert and Sullivan's opera *The Sorcerer* because of the state of his stained hands. While away from Leek, he fretted and became engaged in a protracted correspondence with Wardle about the experiments in colour. This correspondence is described by Morris's biographer, Fiona McCarthy, as being among the most remarkable business letters ever written. Morris became more and more demanding and began to lose his temper. 'They have been very trying: but I wish I hadn't been such a fool: perhaps they will turn me out tomorrow or put me in a blue vat.'

Ultimately Morris was dissatisfied with the Leek experience although he continued working on these problems during the following decade.

They are a number of tangible legacies of William Morris's time in Leek, one being the interest he took in the Leek School of Embroidery which was founded by Mrs Wardle in the 1880s. He offered to design a rug for her woolwork and send items to a textile museum that she created. Fiona McCarthy believes the most moving aspect of his time in Leek is the existence of so many Morris-style church embroidered items - many of them still in use in local churches.

Another monument to Morris in the town was the establishment of the William Morris Labour Church shortly after his death, by Larner Sugden. The art work in the church owed a great deal to many followers of Morris in the Arts and Craft movement. It had red painted walls with stencilled tracery. Woodwork was painted green and the curtains that hung there were blue velvet in one of Morris's designs. Much of the work in the church was carried out from designs by Walter Crane.

The church was the centre of what a local Socialist

author and first principal of the Nicholson Institute, Kineton Parkes, called 'the intellectual and semi-intellectual activity that flooded the town.'

The Church saw many principal figures of progressive politics address Leek audiences through the 1890s and up to the First World War. It was a particularly active time during the opposition to the Boer War in 1899. In October 1899 the pioneer journalist WT Stead came to Leek to speak against the war in his role as a member of the 'Stop the War' Committee. An interesting man, he was the first investigative journalist exposing child prostitution, a cause in which he himself suffered imprisonment. He also carried the first interview in a British newspaper interviewing General 'Chinese' Gordon shortly before Gordon embarked for the Sudan and his martyrdom at the hands of the Mahdi in 1884.

He was also a strong supporter of women's rights and was proud that he was among the first employers in the country to pay women the same as men. He was also interested in psychic research, believing himself to be a reincarnation of Charles II. Stead died on the Titanic. His image was allegedly filmed after his death, which led AN Wilson in his book on the Victorians to remark that the ghostly image of Stead hovering over the shoulder of a clergyman was 'moving testimony to the essential irrepressibility of the fourth estate.'

William Morris was the principal inspiration for the Liverpool-born Walter Crane. They had first met in the late summer of 1871 after Morris had returned from a trip to Iceland. The movement that Morris inspired had many supporters whose work has made an impression on the town, Norman Shaw the architect of All Saints Church was closely associated with the movement. The artwork of William Lethaby Professor of Design at the Royal College of Art in the opening years of the 20th century, adorns the interior of the church, but Crane (a surviving fragment of whose art still exists within the Friends' Meeting House) was a principal inheritor of the Morris tradition.

Best known as an engaging children's book illustrator, he was a forerunner of the art of political propaganda: a tradition that comes down to the modern day. He cut an appealing figure. For their son's birthday, he and his wife dressed up as a crane and a marigold. He was an artist for the new socialist journal, the *Clarion,* at the time of Morris's death and from 1894 he was involved with the Clarion Cyclist Club in Manchester. A newspaper report from the *Leek Times* in 1897 reported that over 400 cyclists from Manchester had cycled to the town on a summer afternoon.

Crane's reputation continued to grow after his death in 1915 and he had many connections with North Staffordshire after 1860. He had worked on pottery design at Wedgwood's and he also painted a number of Peak District landscapes. In 1896 he was teaching at the Manchester Municipal School of Art and, as a follower of Morris, he had also taken the same path to Socialism as Morris had by the 1880s. Both men believed in the importance of architecture as the primary expression of art in a happy healthy community and they looked forward to a future where a united society would create magnificent buildings.

After Morris's death, Crane continued, through the

use of art and illustration, to promote pacifism. He believed that wars were started by capitalists for reasons of exploitation and profit. At the time of the Boer War he was firmly in the camp of the anti-war campaign, judging that the war was unnecessary and a manifestation of imperialism. He was not alone in this opinion. These sentiments were frequently expressed in Leek and at the time of the war there was a very strong anti-war movement, at the front of which was Larner Sugden. Sugden was a man of much distinction and, with his father, had set up an architectural practice in the town by the mid-century.

In a pamphlet published to celebrate the European Architectural Heritage Year of 1975, GA Lovenberry celebrated the role that the Sugdens played in embellishing Leek with many fine late Victorian buildings. He used the quote which commemorates the impact that Wren's buildings had on the capital: 'If you seek a memorial then look around you' to acknowledge the role that William and Larner Sugden played in a similar way on a North Staffordshire mill town in the 19th century. The list in the pamphlet is impressive and includes the Nicholson Institute built between 1882-4; the Police Station in Leonard Street built in 1891; the NatWest Bank and Trinity Church (1863) in Derby Street among others.

During the winter of 1985-6, I remember being on the top floor of another Sugden building - Bank House in St Edward Street - with the then Chief Officer of Staffordshire Moorlands Council for Voluntary Service, the late Peter Shackelton. We looked over the rooftops of a snowy Leek. He remarked that someone should do a book on the chimneys of Leek. Reading through the pamphlet it seems that many of them owe their creation to the Sugden's - father and son.

The Sugdens arrived in the town in 1848, establishing their practice in Derby Street. The younger Sugden was a strong admirer of the work of Morris and met him through their shared membership of the Society for the Protection of Ancient Buildings that Morris help to found in 1877. His admiration of Morris's writings had a profound effect on Sugden. He became a Socialist. inspired by the older man's writings. It was said of him "that it mattered nothing to him that he was alone in his view". Larner Sugden's political beliefs, especially in support of the Boer War, made him a target and his opinions attracted much hostile comment in the pages of the Times. It is suggested that his house at 29 Queen Street was attacked by an angry mob celebrating the Relief of Mafeking in May 1900. Sugden's health was never very strong and there is a suggestion that the strain and the hostility that he faced for his anti-war feelings hastened his early death at the age of 50 in 1901. He was the first person in Leek to be cremated and the first Labour MP, Keir Hardie, spoke at a memorial service at the William Morris Memorial Church in Leek.

Even in the 21st century Morris continues to exert an influence, although it is certain that many people are attracted to him mainly because of his designs rather than his socialist writings. However, in doing this they overlook one aspect of his character that was forged by his experience of Leek in the 1870s.

TOLKIEN AND
THE GREEN KNIGHT

Some time ago I took a party of walkers from Manchester down to Ludschurch from Gradbach. It was a perfect autumn day and at the entrance to the gorge I explained something about the history and myths that surround Lud's Church.

It is a narrow cleft in the rock situated in Forest Wood above the River Dane. The cavern runs for about 200 feet into the hillside and is about 50 feet deep. Stone steps lead into the bottom of the cavern. It is a very gloomy and atmospheric place.

This part of the Staffordshire Moorlands abounds with legends, especially around the origins of the name. One theory is that it is called after the Celtic God Lugh, whose festival is 1st August - Lughnasa. A large flat stone between the river and the ravine is alleged to be a place of sacrifice to the God. And of course there is the association that the ravine has with *Sir Gawain and the Green Knight*.

A recent translator of the poem, the Yorkshire poet

Simon Armitage, feels that the mossy ravine is exactly the landscape that the medieval poet had in mind. I read the passage in the JRR Tolkien translation of *Sir Gawain*, which describes the knight's last encounter at the Green Chapel to the visitors. This is a verse that requires to be read out loud! The encounter occurs towards the end of the poem.

'Then he put spurs to Gringolet, and espying the track,
Thrust in along the bank by a thicket's border,
Rode down the rough brae right to the valley;
And then he gazed all about: a grim place he thought it,
And saw no sign of shelter on any side at all,
Only high hillsides sheer upon either hand,
And notched knuckled crags with gnarled boulders;
The very skies by the peaks were scarped, it appeared.
Then he halted and held in his horse for a time,
 and charged oft his front the chapel to find.

'He urged on his horse then, and came up to the mound,
There lightly alit and lashed to a tree
His reins, with a rough branch rightly secured them.
Then he went to the barrow and about it he walked,
Debating in his mind what might the thing be.
It had a hole at the end and at either side,
And with grass in green patches was grown all over,
And was all hollow within: nought but an old cavern,
Or a cleft in an old crag; he could not it name alright.'

The group were impressed with my not particularly bravura performance and one suggested that the next walk should be around Salford, to give him an opportunity to do a reading from the punk poet John Cooper Clark!

But returning to medieval matters. The 14th century poem starts when a Green Knight arrives at the court of King Arthur one Christmas. The stranger offers a challenge. The challenger must swear that after striking a blow, he will seek out the Green Knight one year hence and receive a blow in return. Only one knight, Gawain, takes up the challenge. He picks up the axe and with one blow decapitates the Green Knight. The headless body comes forward, picks up the head, and holds it while giving voice. Gawain must go to the Green Chapel in a year's time and throughout that journey must always be true. Then the Green Knight, carrying his severed head, mounts his horse and departs. The rest of the poem details Gawain's journey through a desolate wintry countryside to keep his faithful compact with the Green Knight.

It has been known for some time that the anonymous author of a series of poems, of which *Sir Gawain* featured, lived in the North Midlands. In 1817, a local MP, Roger Wilbraham, in a paper to the Society of Antiquarians, said he believed that the poem was perfectly understandable to a 'Cheshire clown'. In the poem, words such as 'bonk, mon, brode, loke, grene, broun dayez, mony, wasch, faytherly, wowes, brek, fode' appear, and these are still used by local hill farmers today. There are also words whose usage has disappeared: bleaunt - mantle, strakande - blowing, clepes - called, schalkez - prepare, lemed - climbed, barlay - respite, trawthe - loyalty and carande - grieving. One word "blench", meaning to cringe was in use until the end of the 19th century and is cited in a glossary of local words in the 1891 edition of Miller's *Olde Leek*.

Tolkien originally translated the poem in 1925 with Professor EV Gordon, his colleague at Leeds University, and he made frequent translations up to his death in 1973. He believed that the unknown poet of *Sir Gawain* was a person of serious and devout mind, but also humorous. The poet had Latin and was well read in French Literature. He was probably a cleric or had some connection with the church. The language, scenery and metre suggested to him that the author came from the North West Midlands.

The creator of the *Lord of the Rings* trilogy was also very proud of his West Midlands associations. In a letter of the summer of 1955 to the *New York Times*, Tolkien described his origins and the geographic inspiration for the books the third and final volume of which was to be published in October 1955:

'I am a West Midlander at home only in the counties upon the Welsh Marches; and it is I believe, as much due to descent as to opportunity that Anglo Saxon and Western Middle English and alliterative verse has a childhood attraction and my main professional sphere'.

And, later in 1955, in a letter to the publisher, Allen and Unwin, he is even more emphatic as to the location of the Shire:

'It is in fact a Warwickshire village of about the period of the Diamond Jubilee - that as far away from that depressing and perfectly characterless straggle of houses north of Oxford, which has not even a postal existence'.

In 2007, Granada Television claimed that Tolkien visited Leek frequently during his work on translating the medieval works. He first worked on translating the poem with a colleague in 1925, returning to it and the companion poems written by the same author, *Pearl, Patience* and *Sir Orfeo* in later translations. The programme indicated that Tolkien visited Leek often during this period, staying at the long-demolished George Inn in Church Street.

I have not ascertained the accuracy of his connections with Leek. However, he did have strong connections with the County as he lived in Great Haywood, south of Stafford, in 1916 while convalescing from wounds received whilst fighting on the Somme. He had even stronger connections with North Staffordshire through his son John, who was a Roman Catholic priest in Hartshill for many years. It is therefore possible that he visited the area during this period, as the first references to Lud's Church being associated with the Green Chapel, to my knowledge, only happened after the publication of a letter by Professor RWV Eliott's to the *Times* on 21st May 1958. This linked the poem with the Cistercian Abbey of Dieulacres beside the River Churnet about one mile from Leek. The abbey was founded in 1214 by Ranulph de Blundeville, Earl of Chester, having being transferred from Poulton in Cheshire as a consequence of predatory Welsh raids.

The anonymous poet of Gawain was a contemporary of Chaucer and was active between 1360 - 1400. It was a time of turmoil in England, between the terrible losses of life suffered under the Black Death - it is estimated that a third of the population died of the plague - and the downfall of King Richard II in 1399. The poem was written while England was involved in a bloody and unrelenting war with France. Gangs of mercenaries wandered the countryside whose actions were far removed from any chivalric code that existed. Perhaps the unknown poet was employing irony looking around at the mayhem and anarchy that was late 14th century England - a situation that Leek was familiar with.

The relationship between the abbey and town was violent in this period. Conflict existed throughout the 14th century between both. In 1379 a commission of inquiry rebuked one William, Abbot of Dieulacres, for oppressing the people and keeping an armed band of 21 men 'to do all the mischief they can do to the people and they have lain in wait for them, assaulted, maimed, and killed some, and driven others from place to place until they made a fine with them'. In 1380, a band of armed men that were associated with the abbey were charged with beheading John de Warton by command of Abbot William. The Abbott was imprisoned, released, and pardoned. No one was found responsible and Warton's death was unavenged. The fractious relationship between Dieulacres and Leek continued up to the dissolution of the monastery in 1538. Professor Eliott, in his letter and in subsequent writings, believed the beheading of de Warton was played out in the poem with the decapitation of the Green Knight. The Abbey also had a Grange at Swythamley, the parish in which Lud's Church is situated.

Eliott believed that the poet was loyal to Richard II who was deposed by his cousin Henry Bolingbrooke and assumed the throne as Henry IV around the time the poem was written. There was a further connection with Richard II, as his father Edward, the Black Prince, had a keen interest in Dieulacres. He died in 1376, followed a year later by his father, Edward III, who was succeeded by the boy King Richard II.

That there are a few geographic clues in this magnificent poem to the existence of the Green Chapel has lead to many claimants for the possible location of the Green Chapel. Earlier, after the encounter with the Green Knight, Gawain leaves the court of King Arthur and journeys westwards.

'All the isles of Anglesey he held on his left,
And over to the fords he fared by the flats near the sea,
And then over to Holyhead to high land again
In the wilderness of the Wirral: there wandered but few
Who with goodwill regarded either god or mortal?'

The Dieulacres connection is further strengthened as the abbey had a number of rights to land in Cheshire and North Wales including fishing rights on the River Dee.

Another pretender for the author of the poem is a member of the Stanley family who also had a very strong North Staffordshire link. The claim is made for Sir John Stanley of Hooton, Knight of the Garter and Master Forrester of the Wirral at the end of the 14th century. The belief hinges on the high number of words of Old Norse origin in the poem indicative of someone who had connection to an area with strong Viking links like the Wirral.

A further argument for the location of the Chapel is made for the sandstone crags above Frodsham which arises from a tradition that goes back to 1547 that the Green Chapel is located in this area. This theory equally fits the topography of the poem with its reference to 'high knokled knarrez with knorned stonez' and it is the nearest highland for Gawain to reach as he fords the Dee.

The poem ends with the Green Knight sparing the life of Gawain who offers his neck to the axe of the knight. He flinches when the axe descends and the Green Knight mocks him. The axe falls again and he receives only a nick. The agreement is resolved. Gawain had been true in all things but one: he had concealed a gift from the Green Knight.

It is a powerful story, which contains many myths. The central presence in the poem is the Green Man, a symbol of fertility and renewal in the depths of the winter journey that the knight makes. Gawain, whose name is associated with the Welsh sun god Gwalchmei, brings back life to the land.

It continues to have a hold over modern poets and readers and in 2007 Simon Armitage's response restored the Middle English alliteration in the original poem. This is a piece of writing that chimes with the modern age and mind with its preoccupation with nature. The poem is the equal of Chaucer or Shakespeare and it is strongly possible that its creator landscape is one rooted in the Staffordshire Moorlands countryside

THE WEAVER AND
THE OLD ETONIAN

'At Leek we rested during an hour, took some refreshment and then resumed the journey towards Ashbourne. In passing through the streets we noticed a number of weavers at their looms and obtained permission to go into the weaving places and see them. The rooms where they worked were on the upper floors of the houses; they were in general very clean; the work was all in the small silk-ware line, and many of the weavers were young girls - some of them good looking, most of them neatly attired, and many with costly combs, earrings, and other ornaments of value showed that they had earned sufficiency of wages, and had imbibed a taste for the refinements of taste... the girls being dressed in a style that two hundred years ago would have deemed to be rich for a squire's daughter, was to me very gratifying; whilst to my travelling companion it was equally surprising'.

These words are those of Samuel Bamford visiting the town in the spring of 1820. The sort of houses he describes can still be seen in parts of Leek today. It says something of Bamford's strength of character that he could make that observation about Leek when other things must have weighed oppressively on his mind. He was on his way on foot to London to appear before the Court of Appeal after being convicted of involvement in the 'Peterloo Massacre' which occurred in Manchester the previous August.

At one point in the proceedings there was a possibility that he could have faced a trial for treason. Such were the times when holding radical opinions could lead to a lengthy prison sentence, or worse. On his way towards the capital, Bamford visited the grave of Jeremiah Brandreth in Derby, a colleague who had been executed for his part in an uprising two years earlier.

Bamford's account of a pleasant April day in Leek appears in his book *Passages in the life of a Radical* published in 1842. It was a widely admired book of its time and he had adherents as diverse as Mrs Gaskell and Tennyson.

Bamford was born in 1788 in Middleton near Rochdale. During the most part of his life he followed the occupation of his forebears as a weaver. The political events that followed the end of the Napoleonic wars were initiated by a Government frightened by the after-effects of the French Revolution. The first decades of the 19th century were hard times of poverty, unemployment and repression. It led to Bamford becoming a radical champion of causes such as granting working people the vote. It was a working class vastly expanded as a consequence of rapid industrialisation. He was present at some of the major political events of the years that led to the demand for deep-seated political change. Samuel Bamford had earlier been one of the 'Blanketeers' - so called because they wore blankets to protest about unemployment and the poor living conditions suffered by the textile workers of Lancashire who had attempted to present a petition to Parliament in March 1817. Many of the protesters were stopped by the authorities in Stockport although about 400 got to Leek before the march petered out at Ashbourne. Bamford's literary style is powerfully descriptive and comes from a man lacking a formal education. His description of the aftermath of the Peterloo massacre in 1819 is terribly moving and evocative:

'the Yeomanry had dismounted - some were easing their horse's girth, others adjusting their accoutrements, and some were wiping their sabres. Several mounds of human beings still remained were they had fallen, crushed down and smothered. Some were still groaning, others with staring eyes, were gasping for breath and others would never breathe no more. All was silent save those low sounds, and the occasional snorting and pawing of the steeds'.

To read his memoirs is to enter a world of long distance hikes through the countryside and of chance meetings. Bamford was a poor man and in order to get to London before the days of the train and cheap public transport, he walked.

This brings me now to the second literary character of the left: George Orwell, who passed through the Moorlands in the harsh winter of 1936. The 100 years that separate the lives of Bamford and Orwell have seen a transformation of the political rights of the population and some of these changes had been played out on the streets of towns and villages of the Moorlands. The political movement of Chartism, which demanded nothing more than a root and branch transformation of the constitution, reached its zenith in the 1840s. A man from Leek was shot dead in the streets of Burslem during the Chartist riots of August 1842. Leek was witness to the demand that women got the vote and principal speakers such as Charlotte Despard came to the town. Regular visitors to Leek in those years included some of the founding members of the Labour Party.

Bamford and Orwell came from completely different social classes and experiences: Bamford, the working class, skilled worker from Lancashire and Orwell, the southern, Eton-educated son of a colonial administrator. And yet there were similarities. Both had a keen sense of the need to address injustice and the ability to use their power of words to tackle inequality and repression. Both witnessed hard times.

Orwell came through the area on his way north. He had been commissioned by the left wing publisher Victor Gollancz to write a piece of extended reportage on the social conditions in the economically devastated north of England. The research would eventually produce *The Road to Wigan Pier*. Orwell, being an observant writer, picked up material that he hoped to use later in the book as he progressed northwards. He passed through the area on foot in February 1936. It was bitterly cold as he came through Hanley and Burslem. He noted in his journal that the streets were full of poorly dressed and desolate looking people. The shops looked meagre and were scantily provisioned. Staffordshire, like Lancashire and Yorkshire, suffered badly during the recession of the 1920s and 30s.

George Orwell stayed a night at the Youth Hostel beside Rudyard Lake. The lake was frozen over and ice had formed into blocks which gave off a clanking sound as it collided. Cigarette packets bobbed up and down among the ice floes and Orwell felt it was one of the most depressing images he had ever witnessed. The Youth Hostel was freezing and lit only by candles. He was so cold that he thawed his hands over a fire in the morning to get warm. He walked on towards Macclesfield, arriving in Manchester, penniless, by the evening. He pawned his scarf and spent the night in a doss house before meeting people who put him in contact with people from Wigan.

AT THE ALTAR OF SEDITION—LEEK, 1817

One Tuesday in March 1817, the horrified people of Leek awoke to find 400 demonstrators had arrived in the town overnight. The group of decent working men had left Manchester to present a petition to the Prince Regent protesting against the poverty and unemployment affecting cotton workers. England, after the Napoleonic War, was in the grip of a severe economic recession.

Many radicals thought the Tory Government of aristocrats was indifferent to the plight of the common man. As they slept rough, the marchers carried rolled up blankets on their shoulders to keep them warm at night and they were dubbed 'The Blanketeers'. The protesters marched peacefully through Stockport and Macclesfield before arriving in Leek.

135

The response of authority was a panicky one. They called out the local Yeomanry under the command of Lieutenant Copeland, fearful of the possibility of violence. The vicar and senior magistrate of Leek, Edward Powys, ordered the detention of the Blanketeers and many were arrested. Local newspapers reported on the marchers describing them as 'subservient to the all too evident design of disorganising society and destroying the constitution'. They were dismissed as 'gaping gulls who surround the altar of sedition made dupes by artful and wilful men'.

What struck me about the accounts was that the condescending language used about the Blanketeers is now used about the anti-capitalist protesters at St Paul's. Melanie Phillips remarked of these: 'The idea that this supremely self-indulgent exercise is a spontaneous protest by ordinary people is wide of the mark. The similarity of these worldwide tent cities suggests that a high degree of co-ordination is involved'.

That comment tells me that the St Paul protesters are regarded, as the Blanketeers were, as gaping gulls made dupes by the artful, unable to make their own analysis or come up with solutions. Something that is forgotten is that the Blanketeers were the beginning a long campaign that ultimately achieved much of what they wanted. The right to vote, a welfare state, work reform and the ability to hold governments to account were all gained. We should recall this when St Paul's protesters are mocked.

THE GENERAL AND THE BLACK NAPOLEON

I saw a puppet Baron Samedi, the voodoo deity, in a garden in Leek. His black top hat was covered with frost. It did not look happy. Later, in a window, I saw a death doll directed at traffic wardens. It suggested that the Haitian cult of voodoo has a toe-hold in the town. It might account for the zombies. In truth, Leek does have a connection with the benighted Caribbean island, in the form of Napoleonic General Brunet.

The early 1800s saw the culmination of a bloody slave revolt on the island of San Domingo, later Haiti. The man who would eventually lead the revolt was Touissant L'Ouverture, known by his contemporaries as the 'Black Napoleon', due to his military prowess. This remarkable man, the son of African slaves, proclaimed the end of slavery on the island and led a war of liberation taking on the French, Spanish and finally the British who sent 20,000 men to conquer San Domingo in 1798.

By 1802 Napoleon was determined to recapture the

137

island and reinstitute slavery. And this is where General Jean Baptiste Brunet arrives into the story. An army, commanded by General Le Clerc with Brunet as a second in command, landed. Toussaint waged a successful guerrilla war against the French, who lost many men through disease.

Eventually both sides wearied of the conflict and peace negotiations were agreed. However, Napoleon still wanted him arrested and Brunet, a supposedly friendly General, drew Toussaint in on a promise of safe conduct. Brunet wrote to Toussaint in the most cordial terms. It turned out to be a trick and he was arrested along with his wife and two children and taken to an isolated chateau in the French Alps.

The manner of the betrayal of Toussaint, in which Brunet played a prominent part, led to a violent uprising which, two years later, resulted in the French abandoning their major interest in the Caribbean. San Domingo changed its name to Haiti and became an independent country, an example of perhaps the most successful slave uprising in history.

As for Brunet, he was captured by the British in October 1803 and arrived in Leek the following year. By 1812 to 1814 he was living in Clerk Bank. He held a weekly soirée, which met in the Sheepmarket. The General had a comfortable life, which has to be contrasted with the humiliation and privation suffered by the man he brazenly tricked.

THE FOUR FOOT RABBIT

Willie the Wallaby was released into the Roaches, a series of gritstone crags, one summer day in 1979. He was a gift of Riber Castle Zoo, Matlock and was set free in the wild in the hope that the declining population of the wallabies would be restored.

The animals had been released before the Second World War by Henry Courtney Brocklehurst who had acquired them from Tasmania. He was killed in Burma during the Second World War. Henry was a keen naturalist and had written about the wild life of the Sudan in the 1930s. His intention to establish a free-range zoo was realised when the first animals were released in 1936.

The wallabies were successful in establishing themselves and the original numbers had grown to about 80 by the 1960s. Initially they found life in the uplands sufficiently to their liking. Unfortunately the harsh winters of the early 60s reduced their numbers. They also strayed off the area and wallabies were caught at Weston Coyney in 1961, at Werrington in 1970 and even as far away as Ladybower near Sheffield. It was estimated that the population was around 20 by the 70s. There was quite a menagerie in the area and a friend's father came face to face with a yak when Ray Baddley was climbing on the Roaches in the early 1950s.

Following the death of Henry's brother, Philip, in 1975, the estate was sold off, with particular interest shown in the Roaches. The 175 acre estate was acquired by two farmers who made themselves unpopular with the climbing fraternity by banning climbing, claiming that climbers upset the sheep. The area had been climbed since the end of the 19th century and many climbers had developed their skills on the gritstone. It was on the Roaches that the two greatest climbers of the post-war years, Joe Brown and Don Whillans, met and established a long partnership. It was arguably the strongest climbing association ever, and the grades of their grit routes have more than stood the test of time - completing a Whillans or Brown route is still a coveted 'tick' to this day.

The land was put up for sale in 1979 and failed to reach its reserve price of £39,000 and eventually the Peak National Park Authority acquired the area in 1980. A character equal to Whillans who appeared in 1978 was Doug Moller the self-styled Lord of the Roaches who bought Rockhall Cottage for £6,000. The 120-year-old cottage was once part of the Brocklehurst estate. It stands at an elevation of 1300ft and is dwarfed by rocks, which gives a breathtaking view of the surrounding countryside. The clash between Moller, the Peak Park and the climbers over access rights was of mythic proportions. Doug was also chopping down trees which was having an environmental impact. I did occasionally see Moller, who was noticeable for his eye patch and for the signs that he put outside his primitive dwelling, which had no running water. On one occasion Doug chased off climbers with an axe which earned him the nickname 'Eugene' after the Pink Floyd track *Careful with that axe, Eugene.* It developed into a David and Goliath confrontation, which would keep the media, both national and local, entertained for years to come.

As for the Wwallabies, the increasingly rare sightings led people to believe that they are close to extinction. Occasionally they were seen. One climber I knew had a close encounter in the 70s:

"I was alone doing some boulder challenges, and suddenly, as if from nowhere, it was there, less than ten yards from me—completely unfazed by my presence. I froze in utter disbelief, tinged with amazement. I wanted the world to stop, or at least go slow just for a minute, but alas, after about 10-15 seconds, even though I didn't move a muscle it turned and slowly disappeared behind a boulder. I walked quickly, and as quietly as I could to the spot where it left my vision, but there was no sign of it".

The existence of the animals led to an amusing exchange on Terry Wogan's Radio 2 show over the stuffed exhibit in the City Museum in Stoke. A family member also recalled an incident in the early 90s. When working at the Leek Road Postal Sorting Office in Stoke he heard a shocked driver one December morning. He reported to his colleagues that he had just seen a four foot rabbit standing beside the side of the A53 near Buxton. The poor bloke was never allowed to live it down.

'ONE FOR THE LADIES'

The wonderful thing about late Victorian newspaper reports is that they carry full verbatim accounts of legal cases with reports carried always in directly reported speech. I came across an interesting headline in the *Leek Times* for 31st July 1897 'Leek Slander Case' and I read on, intrigued. The case was heard before Lord Chief Justice Russell and it concerned a dispute between the plaintiff Frederick Simoni, a music teacher, and Joshua Millward, an auctioneer of Longnor, who also had a responsible position at the Leek Workhouse.

Simoni was born in Italy and had an established music academy, having been a teacher of music in Leek for over 20 years. He had been teaching music for 44 years, the majority of his time teaching the subject in Staffordshire for 37 years. He had a music instrument shop adjourning the *Wilkes Head* pub in which the drama was played out. He called into the pub after finishing work on 10th March 1897. Millward, who was in the pub, began to berate the Italian by saying that he objected to foreigners and accused Simoni of being a 'lascivious man and has seduced his young girl pupils. Mothers ought to be ashamed of sending their children to such a bad man- a foreigner. I know for a fact that he has corrupted his pupils. He has seduced a daughter of a relative of mine and I can prove it'. Millward had made these comments in the smoke room of the pub and had refused to apologise.

The barrister acting for Millward questioned Simoni. He denied being in the pub all day. He had not noticed him until the abuse and did not call him an 'old fool' although he did call him a 'blackguard', but only after he had been badly treated. He had refused to accept an apology because Millward would not agree to it being published.

The next witness was John Gell, the landlord of the *Wilkes Head*, who informed the court that Millward told him that Simoni was a bad man: a foreigner who ought to go home. Simoni had said nothing to provoke Millward. Both men were sober. Millward, when examined by the barrister acting for the Italian, denied making any comment about him being 'lascivious', because he did not know the meaning of the word. He thought that Simoni was 'a rum one for the ladies'. Robert Naylor, a farmer, said that there had been some 'jaw' between the two men. Another farmer, John Hall, said that 'they had called each other everything that was bad.' It was 'market talk' and he took no notice of it. He could not tell who was the first of the two.

The judge felt that, had the language been confined to abusive expressions of a general nature, then he would have only considered it a public-house brawl. But where definite statements had been made which were accusative and directed against the plaintiff's moral character, then Mr Simoni was perfectly justified in bringing an action that cleared his name. It was a very grave statement to make, and could not be passed over lightly. He gave judgement to Simoni for £10 and costs. This led me to think about the career of Signor Frederick Simoni and whether it was possible to construct anything about this man who was well known in the town, despite not necessarily being well liked by the habitués of the *Wilkes Head*. In the manner of the TV programme *Who do you think you are?* I thought I would try to find out what I could of the musician.

What I have managed to find out about Frederick Simoni was that he was born in 1831. He would have been 66 in 1897. He told the court that he had been teaching music in England for 44 years. He was in the country at least since 1853. Trade directories for 1884 and 1896 indicate that he was initially running his music business in Cheadle and then in Leek. In the 1881 census he was living at 2 York Street and in 1897, 18 Deansgate. He indicated that he was married in the census but lived alone at his addresses in the town. He does not appear in either the 1891 or 1901 census. Perhaps he decided to sell up and return to his Italian homeland right at the end of his life.

It is all guesswork on my part, but I believe that Simoni would have arrived in England as a political refugee following the crushing of the Italian nationalist movement by the French and Austrian Armies in 1850. Many of the middle class professionals supported a unified Italian State. At that time Italy was not one country but a collection of states, many of them dominated by foreign powers and the influence of the Pope. People of liberal persuasion supported the uprising and fled into exile, amongst them the leader of the movement Guiseppe Garibaldi. The refugees went mainly to the US or to Britain. Britain was very sympathetic to the cause of a united Italy. In Stoke for example, a street in Etruria was named after Garibaldi in the same way that public buildings were named after Nelson Mandela over 100 years later. Frederick Simoni was almost certainly one of the many young Italians who were forced into exile. Several Simoni's, many of them from Bologna and Emilia Romano, were amongst the most ardent followers of the movement - the 1000 most die-hard supporters. He probably arrived penniless and friendless in London and had to turn to the one thing he knew best, music.

As a music teacher, he would have been kept very occupied, with many of the people in the town wanting to sing or learn a musical instrument. Legions of Victorian girls and young women learned music, as it was considered an essential feminine accompaniment. There were even publications such as the *Girls Own* which catered for the growing number of young women interested in becoming accomplished in music. The magazine provided tips on how to play instruments and included sheet music of popular tunes of the time.

Musical life in Leek was very busy in the 19th century. The Philharmonic Society was established in the late 1830s and subscription concerts were held at the *Swan* in the Assembly Rooms. In 1842 the St Edward Church organist, Benjamin Barlow, in something for a coup for the town, arranged for the German born Joseph Mainzer (1801-1851), a creator of the tonic *sol-fa* singing method, to give a series of lectures in the town. Mainzer's teaching methods were extremely popular and his book, which has the almost modern title of *Singing for the Millions*, had sold 200,000 in the first six months of publication.

Mainzer, the son of a butcher, had trained for the priesthood but had spurned this vocation to become a political radical. He fled France in the 1830s after upsetting the authorities and eventually settled in Manchester, where he established a number of singing classes within a 20 miles radius of that city. He was very popular, especially amongst the professional classes, who saw his methods as offering a distraction to the anti-social behaviour of the labouring classes. He wrote in messianic terms about his methods:

'The time has come when the soldier and the sailor, the plodding labourer and the dusky artisan, will forsake the pothouse and the gin palace for the singing school, and so being raised in the scale of civilisation are raised in scale of humanity'.

Mainzer was in great demand as a speaker and teacher. Leeds tried several times to attract him to Yorkshire to set up singing classes in the City, so getting him to visit Leek often in the 1840s says something of the persuasive powers of Mr Barlow.

Barlow is credited with founding the Leek Church Choral Society, the inaugural concert of which was in 1852. Similarly the Leek Amateur Musical Society gave concerts in the Temperance Hall until 1888 and then held events in the Town Hall after that date.

Sometimes the musicians that appeared in Leek displayed hauteur of almost rock star proportions. In an account of a concert given in the West Street

146

School in 1887, a Mr Hewitson, the pianist, and Mr Dunn, the violinist, kept the large crowd waiting at the Grand Jubilee concert at the school. Hewitson went on to compound the felony by refusing to play a piece because he did not think much of the piano. The *Leek Times* journalist remarked:

'Such affectations and eccentricities are characteristics of many amateurs to which genus Mr Hewitson unmistakably belongs. But Mr Dunn is only at the commencement of his career and will find British audiences are not to be flouted with impunity, and that punctual performance of duties is a *sin qua non* of success'.

After the Nicholson Institute opened in 1884, promenade concerts became something of a feature. A concert given in 1885 was enthusiastically reviewed. The glee party, comprising of Messrs G Crockhall, W Howard, J Lee and FP Walwyn, attempted a new piece by Arthur Sullivan, *The Beleagued* in such a style,

'For it to be re-demanded, but their performance of Hatton's *Village Blacksmith* fairly carried the house by storm, the encore being most enthusiastic; and we hope to have the pleasure of hearing both these pieces performed again at these promenade concerts'.

From reading both the adverts and the reports in press reports, Leek was used to seeing foreigners in its streets in the 19th century. Many of the foreigners in Leek were involved in musical entertainment. Ms Alice Ralphs in the interview that she gave to the Workers Educational Association when they were compiling their *Edwardian Leek* booklet in 1980 records the negro street entertainers. One of them was called 'Professor Tobias' and came into Leek during market events during late Victorian summers. Minstrel shows started in the 1860s and continued in popularity right to the end of the century. Itinerant Italian bagpipe players lodged in the town in 1870s. I wonder if they got into the *Wilkes Head*?

DISRAELI AND THE GREAT HOUSES OF NORTH STAFFORDSHIRE

Benjamin Disraeli was one of the great figures of the 19th century and credited with being one of the founder creators of Britain's imperial power. Born in London in 1804 to Jewish parents, he was always a detached observer of British life and society. His rise to power was difficult, as he did not come from the great houses of the country, which were the traditional breeding ground for grandees of the Tory Party.

Staffordshire made its impact upon him throughout his career. The clash with the Staffordshire-based leader of the Tory Party, Sir Robert Peel — in the 1840s of Drayton Park and MP for Tamworth — made his career. Early attempts to establish himself foundered perhaps because his religion and foppish personality were regarded with suspicion. Disraeli established his reputation through his journalism and his writing. He wrote his first novel when he was 23 and followed this up with a series of political novels of which *Sybil*, published in the 1840s, is the best known. He was interested and sympathetic to the demands of the working class and in his early years in Parliament called for an alliance between the landed aristocracy and working people against the rising power of industrialists.

In 1841 Sir Robert Peel became Prime Minister and his action in repealing the Corn Laws, a tax on bread which benefited the Tory gentry, split the party five years later. During the debate on repeal, Peel was goaded by Disraeli who felt that the landed interests were being betrayed. The resultant divide had the greatest implications for Disraeli as most of the Government sided with Peel and Disraeli was left with a small group of landowners leading the surviving rump of the Conservative party into many years of opposition. Disraeli's first opportunity to become Prime Minister came in 1868. As he remarked, "I have climbed to the top of the greasy pole". It was a difficult and lengthy ascent. The administration was short lived and within ten months the Liberals, led by Disraeli's great parliamentary rival, Gladstone, were returned to power.

It was a considerable achievement by Disraeli in an admittedly more relaxed age to write a major novel - *Lothair*. A novel by a former Prime Minister was a unique event. The book tells the story of a young nobleman who is rootless, well-connected and very wealthy. Lothair becomes a target for conversion by the Catholic hierarchy. He joins the fight for Italian independence against the armies of the Pope and his experience counters any desire to convert. It is an unflattering portrayal of a manipulating Catholic

Church, as well as an attack on an aristocracy which is in danger of degenerating into a useless caste

Lothair has strong connections with North Staffordshire as two of the houses mentioned in the novel are Brentham and Muriel Towers, a thinly disguised Trentham Park and Alton Towers. Trentham was the home of the Duke of Sutherland and Alton Towers that of the Earl of Shrewsbury. The 18th and 19th earls served in Tory administrations of which Disraeli was a member, and Sutherland was an equally a well-known local Tory MP. Alton Towers was built 1811-1820s and the great early Victorian architect Augustus Pugin made substantial alterations in the 1830s. Pugin would later work closely with the sixteenth Earl of Shrewsbury and was much interested in medieval art. He used his associations with Alton to visit medieval churches in the area and the remains of monasteries such as Croxden to inspire him to design one of the great buildings of the gothic revival - the Roman Catholic Church at Cheadle. Another great figure of Victorian design was less convinced. William Morris, on a day trip from Leek, described Alton Towers as a 'gim-crack palace of Pugin's'.

Disraeli however was enchanted by the setting, 'Muriel Towers crowned a wooden steep, part of a wild winding and sylvan valley. At the bottom was a rushing stream. A vast park spread in all directions beyond the limit of the eye, ornate and choicely timbered'.

The first Duke of Sutherland had married into wealth, having inherited vast areas of land in the Highlands of Scotland. The family's name is blemished, as they are held responsible for the Clearances in which Scots were evicted from the land

and forced to move to the industrial towns or emigrate to North America. This compulsory movement of people was done with great cruelty. A huge corroding statue of the Duke on which much blame was directed stands on hills above the Trentham estate. Another one is at Golspie in the Highlands.

Trentham Hall and Gardens were created in the late 18th century. The house was extended and improved in the 1830s by Charles Barry later to be the architect of the Houses of Parliament. New bedrooms were added, as were a sculpture gallery and a 100-foot clock tower, and a grand entrance with portico supported by stone sculptures of beasts. Trentham (or Brentham in the novel) is described as 'agreeable' with long walks into forested ways of 'thick and fragrant scrubs and a dell of high trees and gothic shrines'. Trentham then, as now, is admired for its gardens; huge bushes of honeysuckle and bowers of sweet pea and sweet briars, and jasmine clustering over the walls. Disraeli visited Trentham frequently, staying with the Duke and Duchess of Sutherland following the death of his wife. He spent Christmas 1873 at the house.

The following year he became Prime Minister for a second time, being assisted by a swing away from the Liberals in towns like Leek. His Government was a reforming one and he was able to push through a series of acts, which would help to improve the position of the working class. He died in 1881. His main biographer believes that his sceptical outlook makes him the least dated of all the Victorian figures. There was a champagne sparkle about Disraeli. One has to admire his wit: on his deathbed he was asked whether he would like a visit from Queen Victoria. "No, it is better not. She would only ask me to take a message to Albert".

AN INCIDENT AT ECTON COPPER MINE, 1759

O n 13th October 2010, 33 miners who had been trapped underground for more than two months returned to the surface, after a successful rescue operation that inspired Chile and riveted the world.

The miners travelled up a narrow, nearly half-mile long rescue shaft in a specially designed capsule. The final phase of the long rescue effort took roughly 22 hours, The leader of the group was the last to be rescued.

I came across an event 250 years ago which struck me as having parallels with the Copper miners of Chile. On 20th April 1759, the following extract of a letter was published in the *Derby Mercury*:

'We received an account from Ecton about 6 miles from Leek that the Sough through which men go into the Copper mine had fallen in; there were 15 men in the mine when the accident happened. Luckily there was a cleft in the ground left open which that they received their meat or they must have perished. The Inhabitants are generally employed in digging away at the earth. In order to release them it is feared it will take some time. The Accident was caused by excessive rains they fell on Mondays and Tuesday which caused such floods here'.

Copper mining began in earnest at Ecton at the beginning of the 18th century although the existence of copper had been known about since the Middle Ages. It became one of the richest mines in the country and was considered a good investment as the rival copper mines in Cornwall were prone to flooding. Ecton did not suffer from drainage problems. It returned a healthy return of 40% to the Dukes of Devonshire and the profits were used to develop Buxton as a Spa town.

In its heyday, Ecton boasted of a number of initiatives. Explosives were used for the first time in mining. Boats were used underground shortly after their successful introduction at the Duke of Bridgewater's Collieries. An early use of balance beam pumping engine was pioneered at Ecton, as was the employment of a James Watt rotative steam engine in 1780. The mines were very deep: at over 1300 feet, they were some of the deepest in Europe. A description from 1769 describes how little boys wheeled barrows on the dressing floor, while young girls sorted the ore previously crushed by women with hammers. Wages started at 2d per hour for the children and up to 30d for the men. The age span of workers ranged from five to 60.

CHARLES DICKENS AND JELLYBY

Charles Dickens, whose bi-centenary fell in February 2012, created the character Mrs Jellyby in *Bleak House,* a character so obsessed with helping the poor of Africa that she is neglectful of her own family and community. 'Jellybyism' is alive and well in Leek in 2011, as an exchange I witnessed the other day proved.

I occasionally attend a Tuesday night discussion held in the *Blue Mugge.* It's usually very interesting, although on this night the atmosphere was particularly charged. We were discussing 'Marxism' and someone, mentioning modern poverty, said that it did not exist locally. As proof, he cited the sale of champagne in a local supermarket as an indicator of affluence. Someone else agreed with him, giving as an example of time he had spent in South Africa where real poverty did exist.

But is poverty in Leek easier to bear in 2011 with a welfare state than poverty in Johannesburg? Well, poverty is poverty wherever its experienced. Having no money or support in whatever society is a bitter thing to bear. The only thing that makes it possibly easier to bear is the existence of social support networks and the make do and mend skills needed to survive. If that is the criteria, then who is better placed: a member of an extended family in a Jo'burg township or an isolated pensioner shivering and lonely on a wintry council estate? The number of deaths from hypothermia nationally around 25,000 would suggest a problem.

Besides, I know that there are people experiencing hardship in Leek now. I witnessed an example the other day when I was on an organised walk in the town centre. A homeless man sleeping in the churchyard approached the group, as he did not want to scare people. He told me of his predicament and that he was grateful to the Church for allowing him to sleep there. So, to answer the modern day 'Jellyby', the availability of cheap champagne suggests a restricted social awareness and yes, poverty and hardship is out there.

THE BLACK DEATH

The bones of 16 people recently discovered during the building of the Cross rail project in the Farringdon area of London prompted interest in the calamity known as the Black Death of 1348-50. The plague was a disaster so unprecedented and so great that it engraved itself on the collective memory for generations to come.

The Black Death's origins were in China and the disease progressed along the 'Silk Route' of Central Asia into Europe. The legend is that the disease appeared in Weymouth, carried on board a ship from Genoa in May 1348. Having arrived it spread out quickly, spreading far and wide, ravaging the population of the British Isles for a period of 18 months. Most communities for which evidence exists suffered grievously. Among historians the consensus suggests that a mortality rate of between 40-50% amongst the wider population would not be improbable. The traditional view is that the bacteria was carried by fleas on the bodies of rodents. A modern radical interpretation however opposes this view suggesting that the illness was carried by an Ebola like virus. A series of poor harvests also weakened the general population.

The signs of the plague manifested itself as a contemporary writer describes 'the plague takes three forms. In the first people suffer an infection of the lungs, which leads to breathing difficulties. Whoever has this corruption or contamination to any extent cannot escape, but will die within two days. Another form boils erupt under the armpits ... a third form in which people of both sexes are attacked in the groin.'

The plague arrived in Staffordshire from the South West. It also spread along the River Trent quickly, with Burton suffering badly. In the Archdeaconry of Stafford the first priest died in April 1349. Rents at Croxden and Hulton Abbeys halved, which is an indicator of population loss. In Derbyshire and Cheshire the death rate amongst the clergy took on serious proportions in June. It took 500 days for the pestilence to cover the full length of England. Scotland was so long exempt that the Scots, proud of their immunity, were wont to swear 'by the foul death of England'. In 1350 they gathered together an army in Ettrick Forest with the object of invading the plague-stricken border shires. But the pestilence fell upon the assembled army, and all war was stopped while Scotland was devastated, as was Ireland and Wales. Further plagues visited the country in the 1360s and 1375. Many villages were abandoned, fields untended and churches had no clergy to minister to the people. To the Medieval mind it must have felt that the end of the world had come.

THE DECLINE OF SQUIRREL NUTKINS

My daughter Phoebe is in something of a dilemma. "I like the Grey because we see them on the way to school, but the Red reminds me of a visit to Formby Point". She was talking, of course, about squirrels. The introduction of the Grey, some say, has proved a disaster for the native Red and a species that was wide-spread at the beginning of the 20th century is now confined to the fringes.

I have seen the Red Squirrel at the National Trust reserve near Southport myself and they are attractive critters rendered tame by the high numbers of visitors to Formby Point. The Red, or to give it its Latin name *Scirus Vulgaris,* was plentiful once, but a combination of disease (a major epidemic destroyed many between 1910-20) and the destruction of its habitat have undermined the species. It is likely that the Grey - a Northern American native - first introduced on the Duke of Bedford's Woburn estate quickly spread northwards and were better equipped to take advantage of the changes.

A *Guardian* report of 1912 told how 'large numbers of these grey squirrels have managed to escape or have been allowed to run loose from and in the gardens of the Zoological Society of London, and others have been turned down on various estates. A friend who lives on the edge of a Cheshire woodland not far from Manchester tells me that a large grey squirrel, which looks to him very like the squirrels he has seen in Regent's Park, has paid visits with other squirrels in his garden'.

I don't know when the Red Squirrel became extinct in the Staffordshire Moorlands, but I would have thought some of the woodland around Oakamoor would make an ideal habitat should they return.

Another introduced animal which has also had devastating implications for a native species is the American Mink, many having been released into the wild by animal liberationists. In the late 90s, over 1,000 escaped from a fur farm at Onneley. A resident of Denford told me with some bitterness that a colony of water voles locally had been eliminated, a fact that she blamed on the mink. I saw a mink once by the River Wye, feasting on an elver. These voracious animals are blamed for the 90% reduction in the water vole population.

THE DEATH OF ROBERT PEEL, 1850

The death of Margaret Thatcher has resulted in heated debate about her 11 years in office. The divisive nature of her politics has split the nation, but there can be no doubt that she was a transforming political figure. Her demise and the way in which the news has been regarded bought to my mind the death of another Tory Prime Minister 163 years ago.

In many ways there are many similarities between Robert Peel and Margaret Thatcher, gender aside. Both came from provincial towns, Bury and Grantham, respectively. Both were outsiders. Peel was a representative of the new industrial class - the family had made money in textiles. Thatcher was the daughter of a shop keeper. Both brought success and eventual damage on their own party - the Conservative Party - and both were driven from office by erstwhile allies. The issue that bought Peel down was him changing his mind on legislation that protected the price of bread, the Corn Laws. This policy was bought in after the Napoleonic Wars to protect the income of the landowners who were the backbone of the Tory

Party. Peel repealed the Corn Laws in 1846 after pressure exerted by the highly successful pressure group the Anti-Corn Law League. It split the Tory Party between those who supported protection and those in favour of Free Trade. The divide led to the Tories being out of power for 30 years. Repeal had a dramatic impact on food, halving its price, directly benefiting those on low incomes.

When Peel died in a riding accident in 1850 there was a universal sense of loss especially among the working class. This sense of grief was felt in Leek when a meeting was held in the *Swan* in September 1850 to consider what to do to honour Peel's memory who, incidentally, was a Staffordshire MP - he represented Tamworth.

Mr Doxey, a working man, who spoke at the meeting said that, as a consequence of Peel's Government, "We are in a state of peace, our trade was good, and we are blessed with an abundance with food and clothing within the reach of the working man. We have also our Mechanic Institute where knowledge was cheap and many excellent institutions, where the needy were carried for. He was an admirer of a great man, through whose influences the condition of the poor had so much benefited". A show of hands at the meeting proposed that money raised in Leek should go to the building of almshouses for the poor. Another view outlined in a poster addressed to the Working Men of Leek favoured public baths in the town as had been erected to Peel's memory in Macclesfield. I don't know what happened to the funds that were collected, but around the industrial north there still abound many memorials to the Tory Statesman. Peel Parks still exist in Bradford, Blackpool and Salford.

The Green Knight arrives at the court of King Arthur ready to lay down his challenge. From the 14ᵗʰ century poem highly likely to have been written by someone who knew the area around Leek.

The Great Comet of 1680, described as appearing as a 'fiery sword' in the parish records of Alstonefield.

161

*Early aeronauts such as these proved unsettling
for the people of Cheadle in 1784.*

*John Howard from Leek served in the 51st Regiment at the
Battle of Waterloo and recounted his exploits many years later.*

A BEAUTIFUL, MYSTERIOUS VISITOR

I was flicking through a 1970s copy of the *Post and Times* and came across an interesting tale by local writer George Lovenberry on the opening of the William Morris Labour Church in December 1896. The church - the former Quaker Meeting House - was a monument to Morris in the town and was established shortly after his death by architect Larner Sugden. The artwork in the church owed a great deal to many followers of Morris in the Arts and Craft movement.

The church had red painted walls with stencilled tracery. Woodwork was painted green and the curtains that hung there were blue velvet of one of Morris' designs. Much of the work in the Church was carried out from designs by Walter Crane who signed Morris' obituary in the *Leek Times* the previous October.

The Church was the centre from which, as the first Principal of the Nicholson Institute, Kineton Parkes, remarked 'intellectual and semi-intellectual activity flooded the town'.

It attracted the founders of the early Labour Movement, but it was the identity of a glamorous and elegant woman who attended the opening that intrigued Mr Lovenberry. Originally he assumed the woman was Millicent, Duchess of Sutherland of Trentham Hall, a well-known supporter of radical causes. It was not as a later correspondent, a very young girl in 1896, disclosed. She wrote to the Post *and Times* revealing the true identity of the enigmatic beauty. It was Daisy, Countess of Warwick, a former lover of King Edward VII and a recent convert to Socialism.

The year before, on reading an attack on her and her opulent lifestyle in the radical publication *Clarion,* Daisy rushed to London, leaving a house full of guests to challenge the writer of the article, Robert Blatchford. She explained to him that, during difficult times, the events she held at Warwick Castle provided employment. He demonstrated to his lovely caller the nature of productive labour and the principles of Socialist economic theory. She returned to Warwick in a daze of new ideas and thereafter devoted her wealth and energy to propagating them, to the acute embarrassment of her circle.

It would seem the 1892 popular song *Daisy, Daisy* was inspired by her. The song was famously used in the film *2001: A Space Odyssey.*

HELPING
THE SOVIETS, 1943

I was in a local school looking at a wall chart produced by pupils on the key events of the Second World War. Emphasis was rightly given to the Battle of Britain and D-Day, but no mention was made of the war in Eastern Europe. It's the 70th anniversary of the titanic struggle at Stalingrad, perhaps the most decisive battle of the war - an anniversary that has hardly been mentioned in the British media.

This struggle, in which the Nazis and their allies fought the Soviet Union for control of the city named for the Russian dictator, was one of the bloodiest in the history of warfare, with an estimated two million casualties. The six month campaign, which climaxed in January 1943, inflicted catastrophic losses on the Third Reich, from which it never recovered.

From June 1941, the Soviet Union was an ally of Britain. In Leek, as elsewhere in the UK, awareness of the struggle showed itself in the setting up of an Anglo-Soviet Friendship Committee, meeting at the

Town Hall in December 1941. It was part of a co-ordinated response. The Committee busied itself by running fund-raising events, including a Soviet Medical Aid Fund in the New Year of 1942. Over the duration of the war, meetings with speakers and events were held to recognise the super-human efforts of our Soviet allies. Over two nights, for instance, at Cheddleton Hospital in November 1942, a Russian ballet corps gave a concert.

Perhaps, given the continuing interest in the war, it is right to emphasis that the Second World War was principally fought in Eastern Europe. It has been estimated that 80% of all German allied personnel died, or went missing in action, on the Eastern Front

The vast majority of German divisions were concentrated against the Soviet Union - in 1942, for example, there were 240 fighting in the East and 15 in North Africa and even in 1944, there were more than 200 in the East compared to 50 divisions in the West. The two pivotal battles, Stalingrad and El Alamein, differed in scale by a factor of about ten, on an order of magnitude.

Over 36 million people, 19 million of them civilians, died in Europe in this conflict. The real tragedy was that in Eastern Europe one tyranny was replaced with another.

CONQUERED BY THE TUSCAN GRAPE—THE PERILS OF TOURING

The 200th anniversary of the birth of Charles Dickens in 2012 made it appropriate to revisit an aspect of life that the writer loved — the theatre. I am thinking particularly of the provincial touring company immortalised in *Nicholas Nickleby*.

The Inns of Leek would have seen real life characters not unlike the fictional Vincent Crumles, the actor-manager who appears in the novel. They would have been part of the local scene, especially as improvements in roads made travel easier from the late 18th century onwards. Favourite venues of the actors were the *Swan* and the *Red Lion*. I have seen a playbill from 1843 for a production of *Othello* in the *Red Lion*. In the 18th century, the *Swan* had a theatre at the back of the pub and was used by a number of touring companies. It is thought that the first performance in Leek of Richard Sheridan's play *The Rivals* was performed at the *Swan*.

Its most famous association was with a celebrated 18th century actress, Harriet Mellon, who first appeared at the *Swan* in 1789 and then two years later when the company wintered in Leek. In the late 1790s she broke into the West End Theatre and her fame was assured.

Sometimes things could go wrong and the same venue saw a performance of *King Lear* in 1878 which was bought to an abrupt halt when one of the actresses was accidentally stabbed. Fortunately, the injury was not serious.

A report in a Derbyshire paper in 1850 described a company in Ashbourne en route to Leek with productions of *Macbeth, Romeo and Juliet* and the *Rose of Ettrick Vale* with Mr Thornton, of which more later, 'playing the pantaloon'.

The quality of performance witnessed by audiences of the time can be surmised by character sketches of the actors who appeared in the *Thespian Dictionary*:

Mr Henry Thornton: 'As an actor he boasts of that merit which constitutes a good country performer, for he can bustle through a part with considerable ease, though unacquainted with the author's words'.

Mr George Cooke: 'This actor has experienced both the frowns and smiles of fortune; he is consequently soon conquered by the Tuscan Grape'.

HENRY WAINWRIGHT AND THE SEVERED HAND

Just around from the *Roebuck* in Leek is the Mechanics' Institute in Russell Street. It cuts a rather forlorn figure. It's an early Sugden building, dating from around 1860 and strongly influenced by Ruskin. The lions on the front of the building suggest to me someone familiar with the *Stones of Venice*.

The chronology is right, for the book was published in 1853 and for William Sugden, as for many architects, it must have resonated. I said forlorn and the ground floor 1960s frontage of the building, now occupied by Age Concern, must be the most hideous in Leek.

But first, what was a Mechanics' Institute? They were established at the beginning of the 19th century. They were educational establishments formed to provide adult education, particularly in technical subjects, to working men. As such, local industrialists often funded them on the grounds that they would ultimately benefit from having more knowledgeable and skilled employees. The Mechanics' Institutes were used as 'libraries' for the adult working class and provided them with an alternative pastime to gambling and drinking in pubs. In practice, however, the fees demanded from Mechanics' Institute put them out of the reach of many of the working men of Leek. The Leek Literary and Mechanics' Institute was initially founded in 1837 and it moved to the present location in the early 1860s. It was described as a very impressive structure with a commodious reading room and lecture theatre. It was the only library in town prior to the establishment of the Nicholson Institute in 1884.

One of the earliest speakers at Leek in late January 1864 was a 25 year old Londoner, Henry Wainwright. He was an acknowledged expert on the 18th century poet Thomas Hood and Wainwright spoke on the 'Wit, Whims and Oddities of Thomas Hood'. The meeting was chaired by Lord Norton and the money raised for the building fund totalled £13 7s 1d. It was a very successful meeting.

Wainwright was in a very different situation 11 years later. He had a brush-making business in East London and lived in the Whitechapel Road. Right next door was the Pavilion theatre, where Henry enjoyed socialising with many performers, even inviting them back to dine with his wife. It appears that the younger, prettier actresses were entertained elsewhere. And, when he met a hatmaker by the name of Harriet Lane, he set her up as 'Mrs King' in various East End residences, the last being in Stepney's Sidney Square. But, Henry eventually tired of Harriet's charms. She was murdered and her body was buried under the floor at his warehouse. A year later, in 1875, the warehouse was sold and as it was about to change hands, Henry exhumed the corpse, cutting it into pieces, which he then wrapped in thick canvas cloth. He certainly did try to move the remains, even asking a member of staff to help with transporting them to his new premises - claiming they contained hair for his trade. When the poor workman complained at the stench, Wainwright assured him that it would 'blow off'. A little while later, out in the street, when he complained again at the weight, Wainwright became exasperated, leaving his employee alone with the parcels while he went off to find a cab.

He returned and loaded the packages into the cab and then travelled on alone. But during his absence, the suspicious employee had sneaked a look and discovered a decaying hand. He did not challenge Wainwright at the time, fearing he might be murdered too, but as soon as the cab set off, a constable was informed and, in due course, Wainwright was detained, red-handed, with blood seeping out through the cloth in his arms. There was, however, a twist in the tale. Wainwright was hanged for the crime, but during the court case it came out that he had a brother, Thomas, and Henry had encouraged Thomas to woo Harriet in his place - hoping to make their break easier. When Harriet's body was found, Thomas had long disappeared. Some believe that Henry, having already lost his reputation, sought to protect his brother's name, taking the blame for her death on himself.

Prior to the Mechanics' Institute, cottages occupied the site. In one of the cottages lived a Mrs Yates - an oatcake maker. She was known to augment her supply of wood for her business by stealing from neighbours. They were determined to teach her a lesson and hid an amount of gunpowder in a pilfered amount. The subsequent detonation served Mrs Yates right and cured her of her stealing.

'TAKE TWO LAMB'S TESTICLES'

One of the delights of the summer is eating samphire, the sea-weed that grows in the salt marshes of the coastal regions. You can usually get it in June or July. I became first acquainted with it in East Anglia. It is very tasty boiled and served with lemon and butter. A French lad who was in a group I was camping with thought it was one of the tastiest things he had tried whilst on holiday, a rare acknowledgement indeed.

Samphire appears in the *Whole Art of Cookery* published in the early 19th century by a local publisher in Bemersley near Knypersley. What makes the book unique was that it was published by Primitive Methodists. It was produced in Hugh Bourne's, the founder of Primitive Methodism, own publishing house. The printer was more used to producing prayer books and religious tracts rather than such works of domesticity. However, early Methodists were very keen on personal development and the book had a strong ethic of self improvement which would have fitted with the ethos of advancement. It would have achieved the Primitive Methodist seal of approval, although one aspect of a puritanical religious movement they would have baulked at was the copious amounts of wine that many of the recipes required. The cynic in me thinks that knocking back a few bottles of Sack may have been one way to cope with some of the servings.

The unknown author of the work drew on earlier writings. In the 18th century cookery writers such as Hannah Glasse and Susannah Carter dominated the scene and some of their recipes appear in the *Whole Art of Cookery*. One, for example, was a dismal seafarers dish called 'Portable Soup' which even then was thought to resemble glue. It was a mistake that one of the characters in *Swiss Family Robinson* also made. It might be useful to speculate whether the poor diet of the sailors indicated by the existence of portable soup might be a reason why there were so many naval mutinies in the late 18th century. Another strand that is evident in the *Whole Art of Cookery* is the drawing on earlier culinary traditions of the medieval period, as the book includes heavy use of spices and dried fruit in such dishes as sweet chicken pie or lamb with currants. One item that appears in a number of meals is the oyster. In the early 19th century oysters were the dish of the poor until later in the Victorian Age, when pollution destroyed the oyster beds and drove the price beyond the reach of working people. They appear in such dishes as 'Oysters and pistachio nuts' and 'oyster ragout'. Verjuice is also mentioned, made from crab apples as an alternative to vinegar. In the Middle Ages it was widely used and more recently has made something of a comeback.

Tastes change, especially in regard to the use of

'umbles' or offal, which many turn their nose up at. It was not always the case. As a child I have eaten tripe, chitterlings and pigs' trotters. Many would be appalled at the prospect. In the *Whole Art of Cookery* there are instructions to make 'Calf Head Pie' which includes sliced palates and coxcombs. 'Battalia Pie' requires two lamb's testicles or 'stones'. An essential ingredients of 'hashed calf's head' are 'brain cakes'. The recipe for dressing 'Calves Chitterlings curiously' calls for the meal to be 'closely covered with fire'.

The book includes directions for making wine, elder, cherry and gooseberry wines indicating the range of flowers and fruits that could be turned into semi-palatable alcohol. Home brewing of beer was always a commonplace activity in the 18th century home. Instructions are given for 'strong October' as well as 'small beer' and 'strong ale'.

There are some omissions. No bread or scone recipes are included and, given that it is a North Staffordshire cookbook, no oatcakes.

A SINGULAR CASE ON BIDDULPH MOOR, 1848

The following 'singular' case appeared in the *Morning Post* in the autumn of 1848 concerning a Biddulph Moor woman. On 16th September Doctor Bland, a physician in the Macclesfield work house, was asked to attend a man dying from dysentery who lived in a lodge house in the town. He thought that the man, who was aged about 60, looked decidedly feminine around the face. The man, named John Smith, also had a womanly voice.

The doctor spoke to Smith's wife who was with some of her 11 children. She was not married to him, but had met him 14 years ago in New Mills, Derbyshire. Smith worked as an itinerant knife grinder and spoon maker. His wife said that he was a supportive husband. Some days later, John Smith died and Bland returned to sign the death certificate. His suspicions were correct and Smith was indeed female. The wife told the doctor that she had only found out the day before Smith's death that he was female, when he had implored her to sew the body into a winding sheet. She told Bland that the 11 children had been fathered by her first husband. 'John Smith' was buried in Christ Church and a great deal of interest was shown at the funeral.

After subsequent investigation Bland found that the dead woman had been born Sophie Locke in a cave at Croker Wood, Sutton and moved to live with her extended family who lived on Biddulph Moor. Sophie followed her father's occupation as a tinker and knife grinder. The Lockes were an itinerant lot and spent the year moving around the country, although they always wintered on the moor. From an early age, she dressed as a male and often accompanied her brother around the pubs in Biddulph and Congleton, where the two would dance and play the violin. She appeared to be a volatile soul and pretty handy with her fists. Sophie got involved in a massive punch up at Bolton Green in Lancashire and in the fight a breast was exposed. News of the incident got back to Biddulph and the community impressively kept the secret for the remainder of her life. Over the years, whenever she met someone from the town she became very wary and withdrew from society, although the concealment held. She rarely visited Biddulph Moor after the Lockes were accused of sheep stealing.

She lived as a husband to several women, including one whom she married in Winster Church in Derbyshire. The story is that a serving girl became pregnant after a liaison with a local squire. Sophie was encouraged to marry the woman and bring the child up as the 'father' and this relationship lasted some years. The woman that Doctor Bland met had lived with Sophie for about 14 years and spent the year travelling around the country with Locke and

her large brood of children. Taking part 1
picking in Worcestershire every autu1
something that the family enjoyed.

As mentioned earlier, Sophie gained enjoyı
from challenging men to fight. On one occasion
Bosley, she was making a noise in a local pub. S.
was defying a room full of men, when in walked
hawker from Biddulph that she knew. She exchanged
compliments with the man and then left.

She was described as being dark haired, of wiry build
and very swarthy (that sounds very 'Saracen' to me).
The writer of the *Morning Post* article remarked that
'she would draw the attention of many an admirer of
the gypsy picturesque'.

THE EARLY AERONAUTS
VISIT CHEADLE

A new phenomenon was seen above the skies of
Britain in the 1780s. One summer day in 1785
the celebrated naturalist and writer Gilbert White
roused the locals to view a balloon as it floated above
Shelbourne Church in Hampshire. It was all a new
and wondrous development. The first manned flight
took place in June 1783, when the Montgolfier
brothers launched a hot air balloon from Paris. In the
early days unmanned craft were launched. In
February 1784 one such unmanned craft launched in

Birmingham landed in Cheadle. The locals were unaware of the explosive nature of hydrogen gas which soon became apparent. The *Bristol Journal* takes up the story:

'The farmers took it into a two pair of stairs room, and attempted to blow it up by use of bellows, during which one of the company approached too closely with a lighted candle. The remaining inflammable air tore off the wainscot, broke all the furniture and drove the casement a considerable distance, but did no damage to the bystanders, except singeing their hair'.

The first successful manned flight in Britain took place the following September. A large crowd, including the Prince of Wales, gathered at Chelsea to see an Italian Vincenzo Lunardi set off along with a dog, cat and pigeon. The flight took him to Hertfordshire, where he landed near to what is now South Mimms service station.

Closer to home, a daring aeronaut named Harper took off from Birmingham, rising to over 4,000 feet. He flew over Trentham Hall, descending to ask a farm labourer where he was, talking to the startled man by way of a speaking trumpet. Eventually he crashed at Newcastle and was rescued by a blacksmith as his basket crashed through bushes.

Fairly soon, records were being established in terms of altitude and distance by balloonists. In 1784, the first balloon to cross the Channel landed in France, piloted by Blanchard and an American named Jeffries. One of the first uses of the new form of transport was military. The French used balloons as platforms to observe troop deployment at the Battle

of Fleurus in 1794. Among the troops pre
day was Jean Baptiste Brunet, who much
General Brunet would become the most senior
imprisoned in Leek during the Napoleonic War.

One myth probably needs questioning a
concerns a balloon that is supposed to have landed i
Gun Hill in the 1820s, frightening the locals who took
it for a devil. I am sure that people of Leek would
have been very familiar with balloons from the
earliest days of flight.

A PEAK PARK FORCED MARRIAGE

We live in an age where the thought of forced
marriages and abductions fills people with
horror and reports of such events in the British Asian
communities are condemned. Each year, according
to a recent TV documentary, over 10,000 young
Muslim women are forced into such arrangements
against their will.

The picturesque Blore near Ilam seems a world
away from such considerations, although a dramatic
episode involving a forced marriage took place at
Blore Hall at the beginning of the 16th century.

Margaret Kebell was the daughter of Ralph Bassett
and in 1502 was a 25 year old newly-widowed

woman. She was married ten years earlier to an elderly Leicestershire lawyer, whose death the previous year had left his young bride with a sizable inheritance. In short, Margaret was now a very attractive proposition to the gentry of the area, as any wealth that she had would become the property of the husband.

At the end of January, Margaret became engaged to Ralph Egerton of Wrinehill, who was also a wealthy person, as he stood to inherit lands in Cheshire. A party was organised to celebrate the event. However, someone had other ideas.

On 1st February 1502, an armed band led by Roger Vernon of Wirksworth, Derbyshire assisted by a local landowner, Thomas Foljambe of Throwley Hall, attacked Blore Hall. The brigands arrived at 6am. The band was about 100 strong and was well armed. The trembling guests and retainers were under siege by a group of determined men. Vernon's band broke in and threatened the servants of Margaret Kebell, brandishing swords to get them to reveal her presence. Margaret was found and forced on to a horse and the posse plunged over the River Dove back into Derbyshire. Quickly, a compliant priest was found in Derby and the couple were married, despite Margaret's protests.

Margaret's father was furious and sent out parties to rescue his daughter. Roger Vernon was aware of the threat and moved his new, unwilling bride into Herefordshire until things quietened down. Margaret's mother, Eleanor, accompanied by Eleanor's father and brother, set off in pursuit of the abductors. They were outnumbered and unable to rescue Margaret, but Margaret later managed to escape on her own and reached safety in London. Sir Henry Vernon of Haddon Hall, Margaret's father-in-law, was protesting his son's innocence at court to anyone who would hear that his daughter-in-law was just being difficult. But Margaret was determined to have her say and gained a personal audience with Henry VII.

The case ended up before the court of the Star Chamber, where charges and counter-charges kept the litigation active for many years. Vernon was fined, but in December 1509 all those involved in the abduction were pardoned by the new king, Henry VIII. Margaret did eventually marry Ralph Egerton, who was knighted in 1515. However, whether it was a happy marriage is debateable, as Egerton was reputed to have fathered many illegitimate children.

A WONDER OF OAKAMOOR

I visited the Eiffel Tower recently. It was my first visit. I was staggered by this wonderful piece of 19th century engineering. The design is truly iconic but was deeply unpopular when first erected. However, now, its status is beyond question. Over 200 million people have visited since it was opened in 1889. Closer to home there is an engineering triumph of the period equally as impressive as the M Eiffel construction and its birthplace was Oakamoor.

In the Victorian period, Thomas Bolton's of Oakamoor manufactured submarine telegraph cables.

During the 1850s they were involved in several schemes, but the greatest engineering challenge was to lay a transatlantic cable. The Atlantic Telegraph Company was formed to lay a cable from North America to Europe by 1862. And Bolton's were contracted to quickly produce the copper cable needed.

The first cable was produced at Oakamoor works in 1856. Over 108 tons of copper was used to produce 20,000 miles of cable within five months. It was eventually laid and connected and a message between Queen Victoria and President Buchanan of the US was transmitted on 17th August 1858. However, technical difficulties such as poor conductivity led to only intermittent use.

Undaunted, Bolton's continued to perfect their manufacturing techniques. In September 1863, a new order for 200 tons of copper wire was placed for a second Atlantic cable. Brunel's *Great Eastern* ship was hired to lay the cable and on 27th July 1866 the laying was completed.

Almost immediately, the cable opened for business, but only the rich could afford it - the initial rates were a startling ten shillings a letter, at a time when the monthly wage for a labourer was a few pounds.

As with the overland cables, undersea cables were laid rapidly. Within 20 years, there were 107,000 miles of undersea cables linking the first global communication. The original cables stopped working in the 1870s, but by this time four other cables were laid. It is interesting to note that even though later cables could carry large numbers of signals at the same time, it was not until the 1960s that the first communication satellites offered a serious alternative to the cable, the development of which owes a great deal to the workers of Oakamoor.

WIFE SELLING IN LONGNOR, 1886

In July 1886 the *Leek Times* reported on a wife selling incident in Longnor. It would seem to have been not exactly a rare event. Between the 18th and early 20th century there were around 400 cases of wife selling around the country. An alleged incident took place in 1854 in Leek, so the Longnor case takes such instances virtually to the dawn of the 20th century.

Wife selling was regarded as an alternative way to end an unhappy marriage other than by costly divorce. It was regarded as a rural custom, which relied on the mutual consent of the parties. To give wife selling validity, it was necessary to make it a witnessed event.

Locally, the custom followed a set procedure. A man took his wife to market tied with a length of rope. He paid a toll that gave him the right to sell her. He then paraded her around, extolling her virtues. Once the deal was agreed. the parties adjourned to a local pub and the deal would be sealed over a beer.

The *Leek Times* reported that three tinkers came to Longnor, one was playing a tin whistle, another sang and the third, a woman, collected pennies. A local farmer, John Gould of Coats Farm, Hollinsclough whose wife had left him years before, entered into negotiations to buy the woman. The sale was agreed over brown ale in the *Bull's Head*. Gould then took the halter to lead his newly acquired wife into the market place so that his friends were made aware of his new acquisition.

At this stage a local policeman intervened and the farmer was told that his purchase was illegal and that he ran the risk of being run in. It did not deter him. He said "I do not think you can interfere with me when my wife left me. I have the right to buy another." The couple was last seen walking away from the *Bull's Head* arm in arm later that evening.

By 1886, the practice was dying out and the passing of divorce legislation in the middle of the 19th century spelt the end of wife selling. Before the 1857 Act, a man whose wife had committed adultery was forced to take drastic action such as wife selling to regain their self-respect. It is likely though, that the tradition lingered on in rural areas.

'AS I WAS SO YE BE'

Taphophilia - the study of gravestones - might be considered a gloomy subject, but there are many gems to be uncovered in country churchyards. The Moorlands has a number of excellent examples, which cast an interesting light on the lives of people of the past. In Longnor lies the celebrated William Billings, an old soldier who fought with the Duke of Marlborough at Ramillies and distinguished himself at the Siege of Gibraltar in 1704:

'Billeted by death, I quartered here remain,
When the trumpet sounds, I'll rise and march again.'

If longevity is merit, then there is the tombstone in Horton raised by public subscription to perpetuate the memory of Mary Brooke who died in 1787 at the age of 119, having lived through the reign of seven monarchs. In Endon there is another ancient, Billy Willet, who as a hale young man bragged that he began dancing at "Mester Fordo'yon bonk about se'en o'clock at neet o' the second of September and never stopt whiole daylee to the fourteenth." The trick is that he danced while the old calendar replaced the new on 2nd September 1752, which was followed by 14th September to make up the gap in time.

In Leek Church there is a rare monumental Elizabethan brass to John Ashenhurst with his four wives, not forgetting his many children, dressed in the clothes of the time. The churchyard holds the bones of French servicemen of the time of Napoleon. And there is a *momento mori* from 1749:

'As I was so ye be
As I am so shall ye be
That I gave that I have
That I spent that I had'

In Rushton Spencer, a monument exists to Thomas Meaykin who was buried on 16th July 1781. The inscription reads: 'As a man falleth before united men so fell I.' Two words in the Greek alphabet follow - *bia thanatos,* meaning to die violently.

I have to say, my favourite and very wry memorial is in Suffolk at Bramfield and concerns Bridgett Applethwaite, who died in the 1740s:

'After the fatigues of a married life bravely born by her with Incredible Patience for four years and three quarters bating three weeks; and after the Enjoiment of the Glorious Freedom of an Easy and Unblemish't widowhood, for four years and upwards, She resolved to run the risk of a second Marriage-bed'.

A MAN ON THE RUN—
THE RED LION, LEEK
1836

The *Red Lion* is a fine coaching inn and dates from the 1760s when a toll road to Macclesfield and the North was opened. It has earlier foundations, as excavations carried out in 1991 revealed an older building within the structure of the *Red Lion* from Tudor times. It has had a long history, during the Napoleonic Wars French Prisoners of War gathered there to hold regular Masonic meetings. Along with the *Swan,* it was also a venue for visiting theatre companies. A notice for 1843 from a company performing *Othello* at the *Red Lion* has been displayed in Leek Library.

Manuel Egido da Silveria of Rio de Janeiro disembarked from the Manchester coach a matter of minutes before his death. Mr Brunt the silk manufacturer was worried. The foreign-looking gentleman who climbed out of the Manchester coach looked very agitated. It was midday on Tuesday 7th October 1836 and the mail coach had arrived promptly outside the *Red Lion* in the Market Square. The arrival and the departure of the mail coach were always noted with interest. Mr Brunt and Mr Alcock, the ostler, returned to the *Red Lion* and climbed the stairs to an upper room. At the top of the stairs they met Miss James, the niece of Mr Barlow the landlord, and a serving girl, Agnes Hambleton, having heard what had sounded like a gunshot.

The two men entered the room, which was full of smoke and smelt of gunpowder. In a corner of the room was a toilet, which had been locked from the inside. They tried to force the door. They eventually got it open and lying on the toilet floor was the foreign-looking gentleman with a pistol in his right hand. Mr Robins, a local doctor, was called for, but it was obvious that the man was beyond hope. He had shot himself in the right ear and blood and brain matter oozed out of large hole in the left side of his head. They laid him on the bed in the room, but he died a few moments later without uttering a single word.

Who was Manuel da Silveria, the name of the man who lay dead on a bed in the *Red Lion*? He was Brazilian and a man of some importance. He was described in the coroner's report, published in the *Macclesfield Courier* on 15th October 1836, as being a person who held a commission for the newly-independent Brazilian Government for the West African country of Sierra Leone. In other words, Manuel Da Silveria was probably a person of some influence and connections; certainly the name had a long connection with Africa and Portuguese influence. A Silveria was canonised by the Catholic Church following his murder by Muslim Slave Traders in Africa in the 16th century. Several of that name crop up as colonialists running areas of Asia and Africa for the Portuguese Crown in times past.

The Brazil that Da Silveria would have known would have been in a state of turmoil during the 1820s and 30s as it sought to free itself of Portuguese rule to eventually proclaim, in 1822, the first Brazilian Emperor, Pedro I, to rule an extremely large empire. The Emperor proved autocratic and after an uprising fled to Britain.

One subject that would have linked Brazil and West Africa where Da Silveria worked would have been slavery. The Portuguese had begun to take slaves from West Africa in the late 15th century and slaves were forcibly taken in their millions over the next 300 years to North and South America. By the early 19th century a country like Sierra Leone, by then a British possession, would have been in the front line in the attempt by the British to drive slave trading out of the continent. During the period that Da Silveria worked there, the British launched military expeditions against slave owning chiefs. Perhaps he was ensuring Brazil's interests, still slave based, were defended? It took Brazil several years to take the decision to abolish slavery and then only after considerable British pressure.

A clue about the wealth of Da Silveria emerged at the inquest, when reference was made to him living at a London address and also a Liverpool one. The London address of Portland Place would have been very fashionable in 1836, as the Adam brothers had designed the houses there only a few decades before. In the case of the Liverpool address the area around Great Charlotte Street was rapidly being developed in a city that had very strong slavery associations.

At the inquest, Dr Robins reported that examination of the corpse revealed that the bullet had entered the head of Da Silveria through the right lobe of the ear and had travelled upward causing an inch-long exit wound. Mention is also made of an old injury on the back of the head, which he had complained about to Henry Numes, a personal friend of Da Silveria who lived in Liverpool. The doctor also suggested that the dead man's liver showed signs of damage.

Numes gave a vital clue at the inquest, which confirms Da Silveria involvement in West Africa. He said that Da Silveria had moved to Liverpool only four months before he shot himself in Leek. He was on long-term sick leave from the Brazilian Government after falling ill with a fever in West Africa. He told the coroner that his friend was of a depressed state of mind as a consequence of his work in Sierra Leone.

Another possible reason for the action taken by De Silveria was that he was under investigation by the authorities and the police, accused of a massive fraud against the Brazilian Government. In fact, the Consul General for the Brazilian Government and a man called Ruthven, a detective hired by him, attended the inquest. The matter led to a great deal of interest in the town with over 200 trying to attend the inquest in the *Red Lion.*

A LEEK SOLDIER AT WATERLOO

The Battle of Waterloo, the 200th anniversary of which fell on 18th June 2015, was an epoch-changing engagement that set the course of European history for the next century.

In a field to the south of Brussels, the Armies of Wellington, Napoleon and Blucher fought an all-day engagement with forces of around 300,000 men.

One of the men was 33 year old John Howard of Clerk's Bank in Leek, whose reminiscences of the campaign were captured over 60 years later by a local journalist. Howard was in the 51st Regiment, later to become the King's Own Yorkshire Light Infantry. He had joined the Army two years before and had seen action with the 51st in Spain and France in one of the most battle-hardened units in the British Army.

At Waterloo this was unusual, as most of the troops engaged on the Allied side were untested and inexperienced. Although vastly experienced, the Duke of Wellington led a diverse army drawn from several

191

countries in Northern Europe: along with the British there were Dutch, Belgian and German troops. A third of his troops were under the control of the young heir to the Dutch throne.

Wellington also had to rely on the Prussian Army under the control of the 71 year old Field Marshal Blucher, who was some distance from the British, but with whom Wellington had to effectively liaise, as only their combined forces could beat their common enemy, Napoleon.

As for Napoleon, he had been exiled to the Mediterranean island of Elba the year before. People of Britain had celebrated the imprisonment of the Corsican by holding parties to celebrate the end of a 20 year war. People in Cheadle and Leek at the end of the war in 1814 had led a mock trial and execution of a dummy dressed as Napoleon. But the peace did not last very long and, by the spring of 1815, Napoleon landed in the south of France and marched northwards to take on and beat the Allied forces close to the French and Belgian border.

The Emperor was quickly able to scatter the Prussians at Ligny on 16th June and two days later Wellington faced the French on the slopes near a village called Waterloo. The weather in the days before the main engagement was very wet. The Leek soldier, who had marched from barracks in the South of England and embarked for Calais, was in Belgium within a matter of days. With the rest of the Allied armies, he was in position awaiting the French, having to stand in pelting rain for several hours. He had little to eat save for hard biscuit soaked in water. The 51st were positioned on the far left of the battlefield, near a chateau called Hougoumont which was a key position at a vital road.

The battle began at 11.30am, when a cannonade began to pound the British position. The chateau came under sustained attack. It was garrisoned by a combination of British, Dutch and German troops who spent the day beating off sustained assault.

Howard said of Hougoumont "the roar of cannons, the rattle of musketry, the neighing of horses and the flashes of light all making a sight that I wish never to see again ... Our lancers charged the French they were on them before they could turn around, you could hear the blow of swords on the breast plates of the Cuirassiers and the snorting of the horses ... You could see the man on the ground holding their hands up to fend off the hooves."

The climax of the battle was the assault on the British squares of infantry by the French cavalry. Hundreds of the best cavalry of the world threw themselves against the ranks of the best infantry. The cavalry stood no chance, yet for a period of several hours they hurled themselves against the British squares.

Some of the French horsemen broke away and galloped down a lane to face Howard's Regiment.

"We opened fire the work was done in an instant. By the time we had loaded and the smoke cleared only one individual could be seen running away," Howard said.

As the evening fell, the Prussians began to arrive on the British left and Wellington realised that victory was at hand. In one desperate final attempt to break the British and their allies, Napoleon sent forth his veterans, the Imperial Guard, into the battle. Volleys of fire from Wellington's troops broke the French who fled. Napoleon's cause was lost.

Waterloo cost Wellington around 15,000 dead or wounded and Blucher some 7,000. Napoleon's losses were 24,000 to 26,000 killed or wounded and included 6,000 to 7,000 captured, with an additional 15,000 deserting subsequent to the battle and over the following days.

Howard left the army in 1822 and spent his last years living at Clerk's Bank and mending umbrellas, no doubt telling anyone who wanted to hear stories of his martial valour.

ABOUT THE AUTHOR

Bill Cawley was born in 1955 in Stoke on Trent. He can trace his family back to the 18th century, originating from Cheshire on one side and North Staffordshire on the other. He has always had an interest in History. One of his earliest memories is giving an impromptu talk to a group of American tourists in the Royal gallery at Madame Tussauds when he was six years of age on the monarchs of Britain.

He is passionate about storytelling and recalls sitting in a classroom of over 50 at St Peter's School in Stoke, when the Deputy Head Mr Tipton told stories about Ancient Greece and Rome. The appreciation of a good yarn has remained with him.

After Graduating from York University with a degree in Economic History and Politics, he pursued careers in the National Health Service, Local Government and the Voluntary Sector. He has lectured to Local History Groups and conducted tours for a number of organisations. He has also written for national and local newspapers and broadcasted on radio. He currently has a show on Moorlands Radio on a local history theme.

Bill has an encyclopaedic knowledge which has served him well as a contestant on *Mastermind*, *Brain of Britain* and *University Challenge*.

He is married with one daughter.

ALSO BY BILL CAWLEY

Bill Cawley offers his unique perspective on life on the other side of the checkout - a one-man Mass Observation survey of shoppers who have passed his till.

First published via social media, and now brought to print for your amusement and enjoyment, these anecdotes and observations offer a look at life in the 21st century from the viewpoint of someone who knows his onions and can tell them from his shallots.

"a humorous insight into working in a supermarket and the nation's shopping habits"

ISBN 978-0957314139
£4.99

ALSO FROM LEB BOOKS

Gillian Large began life the hard way in the West
Midlands in the late 1940s.

Although her mother had a wealthy, privileged
upbringing, Gillian was born into an inner world
of squalor and chaos.

In *It's Always the Children*, Gillian takes you on a
roller coaster ride of her early family life in the 50s
and 60s to womanhood with courage, inner
strength and humour.

*"A very honest account of shocking emotional
and physical abuse"*

ISBN 978-0957314177
£11.99

INDEX

43814168R00115

Made in the USA
Charleston, SC
07 July 2015